ELEPHANTS
IN THE TEA

A JOURNEY THROUGH ALS

Barbara Ball

BARBARA BALL

The names of all medical personnel have been changed.

Scripture quotations are from the Holy Bible, NKJV.
Lyric fragment from "Softly," by Shaper, DeVita, Calabrese.
Cover design by Kathryn E. Campbell
Text layout by Patricia Coppedge

ACTS publishers • Portland, OR
ISBN: 978-1-4507-0859-3

For Catherine,
whose joyous spirit shed light in the darkness;
—and still does.

PROLOGUE

$\mathcal{L}$ife was about to change. Forever.

Most of life's changes are sought after, seized, and savored. To grow is to embrace change. From the time a child is born we anticipate change and watch with a mixture of pride and amazement as each change occurs. The toddler's first sure steps give a hint of what lies ahead for they are headed away from the parent. A sure sign of change. That's the way life should be.

But now something we did not seek, something we did not plan, something we could not stop was about to invade our secure comfort zone. It was arbitrary, relentless, and totally unexpected. Our sheltered existence was about to be challenged. Our faith would be put to the test.

Outside of family and work Bob had two passions: photography and books. Now and then, on a sunny Saturday morning, he and I would stop at a garage sale advertising cameras or photographic items, where he searched for that elusive Leica—the one with a twenty-dollar price tag. If the weather did not favor outdoor activity, we'd often browse through our favorite used bookstore searching for a treasure.

It was on such a dreary day that he uncovered a dog-eared leather Bible in the musty-smelling shop. Printed in the late 1800s, the well-worn edition seemed to call his name. He picked it up and put it down twice before parting with a dollar, the price penciled on the flyleaf. Back in the car I began to thumb through the pages when a slip of paper fell out. I picked it up carefully, since it appeared to be as old as the Bible in which it nestled. I glanced at the words and then read them aloud as we drove down the road.

> GRANT, O, my God,
> That neither the joys
> Nor the sorrows
> Of this present time
> Shall have visited my heart in vain.
> Make me wise and strong
> To the performance
> Of immediate duties,
> And ripen me by what means
> Thou seest best for those that lie beyond.
>
> *Anonymous*

CHAPTER 1

The numbers on the bedside clock glowed bright red: **5:35.**

Nothing stirred. Next to me, Bob, curled in a fetal position, gently snored. Whatever jarred me into wakefulness hadn't disturbed him. Well, I wasn't about to. I gently stretched, savoring the cozy comfort of a warm bed. Hoping to catch a few more minutes of shut-eye, I snuggled under the covers and closed my eyes. Nope. Wasn't gonna' happen. Fully awake, I stared at the patch of sky visible through the clerestory window as it slowly turned from hazy gray to brilliant blue.

Ah, a day of blue skies.

A day exploding with sunshine.

Another spectacular day.

Ho-hum.

Welcome to "La-La Land."

When we arrived in Southern California two-and-a-half years earlier, each day was like a wondrous gift. Unbelievably blue skies, gentle breezes, cool nights, warm days. In this little enclave just north of Los Angeles, the ocean breezes not only cooled us but kept the infamous smog away.

Those same ocean breezes quickly dispelled any thoughts of spending leisurely evening hours guzzling lemonade on a warm patio. The house was not air-conditioned; didn't need to be. Oh, the afternoons were warm enough, even hot at times, but the evening and early morning hours were cool. Downright chilly. I quickly learned to dress in layers that could be easily discarded and retrieved as the day progressed.

In this perfect growing climate, farming prospered. Two blocks away sat a large acreage. Growing season lasted all year, with something always ready for harvest. It fell into its own comfortable cycle: plant, cultivate, harvest, plow; plant, cultivate, harvest, plow. At least three times a year farm workers carried out this ritual. I always thought the ground had to sit fallow for a season between plantings, but the progression never seemed to stop.

When the celery harvest started, the whole neighborhood was perfumed with the smell of celery. With the plowing came the fine brown dust. No matter how often you cleaned, a light brown film covered everything. It seeped in through the doors and windows even when they were shut. It clung to your hair and coated your car. You could taste it and feel it. When the wind blew you could see clouds of brown dust whirling in the air like a living thing.

I stared up at the patch of blue visible through the high window. At the start when we wakened to such a day, especially a Saturday, one of us would exclaim, "Oh, look at that sky! What a gorgeous day! Let's do something."

Having lived in the Pacific Northwest for thirty-some years, we had grown accustomed to gray skies and endless drizzle. Not really rain, just perpetual drizzle. In winter the appearance of the sun was unusual. When the phenomenon did occur, it was *carpe diem*.

Everything else could wait.

Chores? Later.

Get out! Enjoy the illusive sun and cloudless skies!

But, after two-and-a-half years in this land of *faux* seasons, a sunny day was, well, just another day. I often yearned for a gray, cold, rainy day. A pot-roast day.

I quietly eased out of bed, careful not to disturb Bob, showered, dressed, and peeked back towards the sleeping giant. One half-mast blue eye gazed back at me. I plopped down on the covers, leaned over, and planted a kiss on his cheek.

"Good morning!" I chirped cheerfully.

"Hmmm," he grunted, not opening his mouth.

"Love you." I kissed him again. "Gotta' make some coffee," I added as I scooted off the bed. I heard Bob get out of bed as I headed for the kitchen.

Soon he joined me, dressed for work, wearing a starched white shirt, blue paisley tie tied in a perfect Windsor knot, and navy blue suit, with the jacket laid carefully on the bed to be retrieved after breakfast. He had been a thirty-six waist for so many years it was with great reluctance he finally acknowledged the need to switch to a thirty-eight. Even so, at a little over six feet, he carried his one hundred eighty-five pounds without appearing overweight. His fine, blond hair had been steadily receding since college. Now, at fifty-five, he had resorted to that hair cross-over thing men do, combing his thinning hair precisely across the top of his head in an attempt to conceal the growing baldness.

"You want an egg this morning?" I asked, as I poured hot coffee into the mug at his place.

"No, just juice and cereal."

I sat down in the chair next to him.

He automatically reached for my hand, a practice begun when the children were small, gave thanks for our food, and added, "Give us wisdom for the day ahead."

He switched on the news. We ate in comfortable silence. We were not morning chatterers. It took me at least two cups of coffee to really wake up, and Bob usually mulled over the day ahead, often with his day-planner open on the table as he downed his breakfast.

We didn't need to speak; we were content just to be near each other. To my surprise, when he finished his cereal he turned off the news. I looked at him quizzically. He hesitated, then said, "I'd like you to make a doctor's appointment for me."

Red flag.

We had been married for thirty-four years and dated off-and-on for six years before getting married. After forty years I knew this man very well. Doctor's offices, hospitals, and clinics, were places to avoid. You didn't go there unless you had blood gushing from some part of your anatomy, or a hacking cough that lasted for weeks, or a pain that wouldn't go away, or a lump, or something broken. Appointments were seldom made voluntarily and never out of the blue. Bob did not go to the doctor without prodding from me.

"What's wrong?"

"Well, I don't know."

"What do you mean, 'you don't know'? I have to tell the doctor something. What symptoms do you have?"

He could not meet my eyes. He looked at his left hand. "I've lost the strength in my left hand."

Bob was dominantly left. He did everything with his left hand. His right hand was only there for aesthetic balance and to offer minimal assistance in those activities demanding two hands. I said nothing, waiting for him to elaborate.

"It started with my thumb and finger." He touched the tip of his left thumb to the tip of his index finger. "One morning I got up, and I couldn't get my ring off. I always take it off before my shower." He fingered the college ring he wore on his right hand. "That morning at work I had trouble using the stapler and squeezing the wire handles on those largesize paper clips. You know what I'm talking about?"

I nodded. "How long has this been going on?"

"About a month. Last night on the news they did a segment

about a woman. She was in a wheelchair. Do you remember it?"

I shook my head. "No." My voice sounded far away.

Bob continued, "She had ALS, Lou Gehrig's disease. She said one morning at work she went to get a drink and couldn't turn the handle on the watercooler. She described the symptoms I'm having."

"Symptoms? Something more than weakness in your left hand?"

"Well, it sounds weird, but I feel these funny tics in my left arm."

"What do you mean?"

"Sort of like a spasm, a twitching," he replied. "It's happening right now. I don't know if you can feel it."

I placed my hand on his upper arm. Something jumped under my touch.

A twitch.

A muscle jerk.

I moved my hand to his lower arm. Same thing. There didn't seem to be a consistent pattern, just irregular explosions under my fingertips. The constant flutter was easily felt through his shirt.

"Do you feel it?" he asked.

I nodded. "How long have you felt this?"

"About the same. About a month."

"Is it like this all the time?"

"Pretty much. Sometimes I don't notice it."

"Is it painful?" I questioned.

"No, not at all."

"Why haven't you mentioned it before?"

"I, ah, didn't know what to tell you until last night."

"If I can get you an appointment today, can you go?"

"I'll go anytime."

I knew he was worried. "I'll call you as soon as I find out when they can get you in. You want to see Dr. Hedstrom?"

He nodded. We got up from the table. He put his arms around me and held me close to his chest. I tried not to feel the flutter in his arm.

"I love you very much," he murmured softly.

As Bob finished getting his things together for work, I cleared off the breakfast table and automatically cleaned up. I kissed him goodbye and promised to call as soon as I found out about an appointment. I stood in the doorway and watched him drive off. The doctor's office didn't open for another forty-five minutes.

◆ ◆ ◆

The back yard of my childhood home shimmered with yellow. Clumps of daffodils and narcissus waved over a sea of tiny blue hyacinths. Above them branches of forsythia arched gracefully, heavy with golden blossoms. It was the shoulder season. Sweater weather. Not warm enough for bare feet but I tried anyway. Yanking open the screen door, I hollered before it had time to slam shut, "Is it time yet?"

No answer.

I walked into the kitchen. The kettle on the gas burner boiled furiously. Carefully, I peaked inside. The water was almost gone. I turned the burner off.

"Mom! The water's boiling!"

No answer.

A faint whirring sound filtered into the kitchen. Of course. I ran up the stairs to the fireplace room. There she sat, hunched over the sewing machine. The machine seemed to be a natural extension of her body, like an arm or a leg. Part of her. When she was creating something, she slipped into another world. Whether she was making a dress or a skirt on the machine, crocheting a tablecloth, or working at the loom on a hooked rug, she was gone. The here and now disappeared. The dock furniture could float away in the midst of a Nor'easter. Lightning could strike the chimney.

The dog could throw up at her feet. She'd barely notice.

"Mommy! The water's boiling!"

With an effort, she tuned into my words. "Oh. Turn it off, would you, dear? It's for tea. I'll be done in a minute."

Even when she was working on a new pattern, there was usually a cup of tea within reach. Mama loved her tea. Hot in the winter, iced in the summer. Once she confided that her secret dream was to have a lunch room, a tea room called The Copper Kettle.

She'd serve cucumber, cream cheese, and watercress sandwiches with the crusts cut off; scones with homemade grape jam; light-as-a-feather popovers; all kinds of muffins; butterfly cupcakes with lemon filling; crispy cookies; and gourmet teas. She already had the copper kettle, complete with dents. When she talked about it, her eyes grew bright, her cheeks flushed, and then, almost embarrassed that she had shared a private dream with me, she sighed, "Someday. Maybe."

At dinner time Mama always made tea for the grown-ups. She would carefully measure loose tea into the teapot and then fill it with rapidly boiling water. She would allow it to steep for a few minutes before pouring it through a strainer into the teacups. If she thought the tea leaves had settled sufficiently, she would pour the tea directly into the cup without using the strainer.

Sometimes just the act of lifting the teapot would disturb the leaves and a few would escape into the cup. If Daddy happened to drink an elusive tea leaf he would invariably say, "Kack! Elephants in the tea!"

One evening after hearing him make such a claim, I asked, "Daddy, why do you always say that? There are no elephants in your tea!"

"Well, it feels like an elephant."

"But it's only a tiny tea leaf!" I protested.

"It may look like a tiny tea leaf, but when it gets stuck in the back of your throat, it feels like an elephant."

My sister and I giggled. Daddy pretended not to be amused. From then on we referred to anything that interfered with the normal or expected flow of life as an "elephant in the tea" event.

◆　◆　◆

An elephant in the tea. The memory of that phrase came tumbling back into my train of thought and even though I didn't know it yet, there *was* an elephant in the tea. It lurked at the bottom of the teacup just waiting to get lodged in my throat and all the "kacking" I could generate would not be able to dislodge it. I stared after the departing car and caught myself praying out loud, "Please, Lord, let it be something else, not Lou Gehrig's."

CHAPTER 2

*A*lternately pacing and standing motionless in the middle of the family room, I waited for the doctor's office to open. Staring not seeing.

This won't do. Let's see, what do I know about Lou Gehrig's disease? Nothing. Well, hardly anything. I knew who Lou Gehrig was. Even as a child I was a rabid Yankees' fan. I remember the day Gehrig gave his farewell speech and the impact it had on those around me. I knew he died from ALS, a disease that would forever after be called by his name. That was about it.

I hurried into the small room we used as a den and looked for the medical reference book. It was so big I had to use two hands to take it down from the shelf. I don't remember where we got it, probably at a garage sale or some second-hand bookstore.

I turned to the back and looked up Lou Gehrig.

Not there.

I looked up ALS.

Not there.

I looked up Am... something or other. I didn't even know how to spell it and I wasn't sure how to pronounce it, but I figured there would be three words beginning with the letters A, L, and S.

Not there.

Okay, so we're dealing with something that's not a run-of-the-mill disease.

I put the medical reference tome back on the shelf, grabbed the health reference volume we had gotten from *Reader's Digest* and turned to the index at the back.

No Lou Gehrig's.

No ALS.

No Am... something or other. *Ah, come on!*

In desperation, I pulled down old reliable *Webster's*. There it was. *Lou Gehrig's disease—Am. baseball player who died of this disease: AMYOTROPHIC LATERAL SCLEROSIS.*

When all else fails, reach for Webster. Now at least I knew how to spell it. I looked it up: "a rare progressive degenerative fatal disease affecting the spinal cord, usually beginning in middle age, and characterized especially by increasing and spreading muscular weakness called also Lou Gehrig's disease."

Fatal. It didn't say sometimes, or often, or usually, just fatal. Did it really mean fatal? Oh, Lord, please let it be something else.

I glanced at my watch. *Almost time.* Maybe my watch was running slow. I picked up the receiver and dialed the number.

"The office will open at 8:45. Please call back after that time."

I hung up the receiver and paced back and forth. I'd never seen the hands on the clock move so slowly. I felt my arm. No twitches. Bob had felt them for a month and didn't tell anyone. I called the doctor again. This time someone answered.

"Hi, I'd like to make an appointment for my husband to see Dr. Hedstrom."

"For what?"

"He's, ah, he seems to have lost the strength in his hand."

Pause. "Can he come in at 3:15 this afternoon?"

Oh, thank you, Lord. Today, they could see him today. We made arrangements, and I called Bob at work.

"Hi, Hon. I talked with the clinic and made an appointment for

3:15 this afternoon. Can you be there?"

"I'll be there."

The conversation was brief. We hung up. I stared out the window. Why did I have this feeling of dread? Because it was Bob, my love, my friend, my soul mate, my life.

◆　　◆　　◆

We were fifteen when we met. That's what we remember. We first met when we were about four. Our families attended the same church where we lived in North Jersey, and Bob and I were in the preschool Sunday School class. All the chairs in the room were painted the same color, with the exception of one chair painted red. The birthday chair, I suppose. Since our birthdays are a week apart, we apparently fought over who got to sit in that chair. I say apparently because neither of us could remember such an incident but our mothers frequently reminded us. Perhaps it was a veiled warning that we were too competitive to ever get along, but, knowing my mother, it was probably meant as an omen that early on we were destined for each other.

My family moved to South Jersey when I was five, and Bob and I didn't see each other for the next ten years. Then we moved back to North Jersey. We moved during the summer months but the full impact of that change didn't hit until school started.

Transferring to a new school is, at best, awkward. During the teen years it can be downright traumatic. All the cliques are in place, and some kids have been together since kindergarten. Unless you happened to be a knockout cheerleader type, you made about as much impact as a drop of water on a rainy day.

I remember walking into the new school that first morning

of my junior year, finding my homeroom, and feeling relieved to see somebody I knew: Bob (that church thing again).

Everybody was assigned to a homeroom. We gathered there each morning before class, took attendance, listened to announcements, and generally visited. We were a diverse group. All on different tracks, all with different class schedules, and, once the bell sounded for first period, we seldom saw each other the rest of the day.

I probably overdid it, but I was really glad to recognize someone, anyone. How Bob and I happened to be in the same homeroom was mere coincidence, or was it Providence? As it turned out, we saw a lot of each other, visiting every school-day morning in homeroom and again at church on Sunday.

It was love at first sight for Bob. I thought he was boring (which he wasn't), too skinny (which he was), homely (he was still in that gawky teen phase), and lovesick (which he was). But … his eyes, oh, his eyes! Great pools of blue you could almost drown in. And his voice. He had a drop-dead bass voice, and he loved to talk—even to adults which endeared him to my parents.

Most of the teen-age boys who followed me home had difficulty stringing two words together and could only grunt or respond with a one-syllable answer when asked a question. Bob's ability to actually carry on a conversation with an adult made him instant dating material in the eyes of my mother. Of course, Mom's endorsement immediately made him less desirable in my eyes. You know, that rebellious teen thing. Just as well; at fifteen we weren't ready for commitments.

The summer we were sixteen things changed. On a warm, sultry evening we went roller skating with the youth group from church. Afterwards Bob walked me home. Mom, always delighted to see him, fixed us some lemonade, and we sat at the kitchen table playing checkers.

"Man! It's hot. Let's go for a walk."

With Mom's approval, we headed outside and down the front steps. After a leisurely stroll around the block, Bob said, "It's too nice to go in yet. Want to sit on the back steps?"

It was still humid out. Growing up on the East Coast, we were accustomed to humidity–the kind of muggy heat that made you want to get back in the shower fifteen minutes after getting out. It felt heavy and thick, and, on days when it was unusually high, it seemed to push you into the ground. No matter how starched and ironed you started out, by the end of the subway or bus ride you looked wretched. When the sun finally went down, it got a little cooler. But many a summer night was spent lying on top of the sheets, unable to sleep, waiting for it to cool down, waiting for the humidity to decrease, waiting for morning to come.

We sat on the back steps. The moon was full, the stars shimmered and an occasional firefly lit up the backyard with a momentary gleam. The only sound was a chorus of a thousand crickets.

"Nice night," I murmured.

At the same moment, I felt Bob's hand on my shoulder. As I turned to look at him, he kissed me–a kiss of infinite tenderness and passion. That was it. Everything stopped. My toes curled. The back porch started spinning. Angelic choirs sang. The stars turned into celestial fireworks.

In that instant I knew we were destined for each other. No one would ever kiss me like Bob did. Years later Bob would tell me his feet never touched the ground when he walked home that night.

Life with Bob may have been a foregone conclusion, but I wasn't ready to accept the inevitable. Surely there must be someone else meant for me instead of this tall, skinny teen-ager. During the next six years, we dated, fell madly in love, broke up, dated other people, started dating each other again, broke up, got engaged to other people, broke that off, and on, and on, *ad nauseum.* An undeniably on-again and off-again relationship. No wonder his mother thought I was just stringing him along.

It took six years for me to realize I was hopelessly, passionately in love with Bob, and if I didn't marry him I'd always have to cross to the other side of the street if I saw him coming towards me hand-in-hand with someone else. Finally, during our senior year of college, we got engaged again, but this time to each other. In spite of our up-and-down romance, when we did marry it would be forever.

◆　◆　◆

The shrill ring of the phone broke into my thoughts. I glanced at the clock as I hurried to answer it: 4:00 p.m. Could Bob be back from the doctor's already?

"Hello?"

It was Bob.

"Just to let you know, I'm back."

"What did the doctor say?"

"Listen, I've got a call holding. I'll see you tonight."

The phone went silent. Clearly he didn't want to talk about it, or he didn't want anyone at work to overhear him. I'd have to wait 'till he came home.

"Well?"

We had gone for a walk. I knew after all these years to give him space. If Bob wanted to discuss a heavy subject, we'd go for a ride, go out to dinner, go for a walk, or sometimes just wait until we got into bed and the lights were out. I suppose it seemed less serious or less confrontational if you didn't have to make eye-to-eye contact. On the other hand, it just might have been an attempt to keep our comfortable surroundings free from possible strife.

He was silent for so long I thought he wasn't going to tell me anything. I tried again, "Did the doctor give you any idea of what it might be?"

"Nope. He ran a series of tests, took about a gallon of blood, well, just shy of a gallon." He smiled. "Seemed like an awful lot."

"Do you know what he was looking for?"

"You know, I think he was trying to rule things out rather than find something. Checking to see if I'm anemic, if there might be any unusual chemicals or some type of metal poisoning in my system. He was also going to have the lab check for things like rheumatic fever or something inflammatory like arthritis. The office should have the results back in a week to ten days."

"Did he do anything besides take blood?"

"Oh, yeah. All the regular things: listened to my heart, lungs, looked in my ears." He cocked his head to one side and raised his eyebrows. "I suppose it has been a long time since I had a physical. He had me do some different things, too."

"Different?"

"Yeah, touch my finger to the end of my nose, turn my hands back and forth." He demonstrated, flipping his hands over and back. "Squeeze his fingers with my hand, close my eyes and hold out both arms in front of me. Everything but stand on my head."

I'd been a school psychologist long enough to know those activities were all part of a neurological evaluation. Casually I asked, "What'd he say about that?"

"It might be neuropathy, whatever that is. He, uh, felt the twitches in my arm."

"Did he say what they were?"

"He said something about 'vasiculations,' but it wasn't his area so he wants me to see a neurologist."

"A neurologist? Why would he recommend a neurologist? Vasiculations sounds vascular. Did he tell you why he wanted you to see a neurologist?"

"I'm not sure. Something about a nerve conduction test. He said this guy, Baxter, is very good. Kind of a hotshot, but he often makes diagnosis that have eluded everyone else and he's usually correct."

"Do I need to make an appointment for you?"

"He made it for me. I have an appointment in a couple of weeks."

Bad sign. Doctors seldom made appointments for you unless they thought there was something serious going on outside their field of expertise. I cautiously asked, "Did you say anything to him about your suspicions? About, ah, Lou Gehrig's?"

He didn't answer for a long time, just stared off into space as we continued walking. Finally, he said, "I told him about seeing the news segment last night on TV and the similarity of symptoms. The questions I had that this might be ALS. I suppose that's why he referred me to a neurologist. Look, I don't want anyone to know I'm seeing a doctor. This may turn out to be something quite simple. No sense in getting everyone concerned until we know for sure what it is. Let's talk about something else."

He had shut down. Bob was always able to compartmentalize his life. He seldom discussed work at home, especially when the children were young. Now that they were grown and gone he shared more of his day with me. Even then, if I asked too many questions he would shut down, saying, "I really don't want to rehash the events of the day when I come home. I just want to enjoy being with you." How could I argue with that?

We walked in silence. Somehow we both knew. He had Lou Gehrig's.

CHAPTER 3

The next two weeks seemed to crawl. We got the report back on the blood work. It was, as the nurse at the office told me, unremarkable. Medical jargon for normal.

Normal.

That's what we wanted.

Everything normal.

So, life went on. Bob went to work each day. Kept appointments. Joked with his secretary. Handled emergencies. Made decisions. Went to church. Talked and laughed with the children when they called. Took the car in for service. Watched TV. Laughed. Made plans for a family vacation at Sunriver. Walked every evening. Did all the normal things.

We didn't mention the specter of ALS, but it hung between us like a thick gray cloud. The strength in his hand seemed to come and go. Some days were better than others.

"Bob, I need to find out about ALS. Do you mind if I do some research?"

He shrugged, gesturing with his hand, "Not at all; do as much research as you like. Find out all you can. Just one thing."

"What's that, Hon?"

"Don't tell me about it."

I went to the library. I don't remember the names of all the reference works I plowed through. I didn't understand much of the technical jargon. What I did understand was horrifying.

ALS attacks the nerve cells (motor neurons) and pathways, the upper neurons running from the brain and the lower motor neurons originating in the spine. Although it usually starts with localized muscle weakness and wasting, it eventually affects all the muscles. When the pathways deteriorate, the motor neurons can no longer use them to get messages or nourishment to the muscles. Since the muscles have no nourishment, they atrophy (waste away).

The early symptoms of the disease appear capricious: weakness in the legs evidenced by stumbling and tripping over things, or weakness in the arms (hands) evidenced by difficulty with writing and buttoning, or complications with swallowing and speaking. No matter what the early symptoms, in the final stages the patient is totally paralyzed, unable to move, unable to swallow, unable to speak, unable to breathe. Unlike other forms of paralysis, the senses are not affected. The patient *feels* everything but is unable to respond. If a fly crawls on your leg, you feel it and see it, but can't move to shoo it away. The intellect is never affected. The mind remains sharp to the end. Like a spectator watching a losing football team, you watch your body slowly die and can't do a thing about it.

The twitches he felt in his arm were fasciculations not vasiculations as we thought the doctor said. I had this image of a wee Pac-Man running rampant through his body, looking for the nerve cells and severing the pathways to the muscles.

A disease with no known cause.

A disease with no known cure.

A disease with no known treatment.

A devastating diagnosis. It was a death sentence.

I felt nauseous. I shut the book, went home, and tried to block it out of my mind. I didn't tell Bob what I'd read.

Later that day, I looked in the phonebook for ALS. I don't know what I expected to find; maybe they had some kind of listing. To my astonishment, the national headquarters for the ALS Association was just over the hill, within ten miles. I had no idea what I was going to say, but I dialed the number.

"ALS Association."

I went blank. What should I ask? If I said ALS would it make it real? When the voice said "Hello?" for the second time, the words came tumbling out. "Uh, my husband has lost the strength in his hand. And, ah, ah, the doctor has referred him to a neurologist. And we think he has ALS." The last words came out in a rush. I felt as if I were sitting somewhere else in the room watching a stranger on the phone babble incoherently. My hands were clammy. What was I doing?

"You know," I heard a calming voice say, "there are over a hundred neurological diseases. It's very unlikely that he has ALS."

"Well, he has twitches in his arm, and he saw this segment on the news about a woman who had ALS and she had the same symptoms he's having."

I was rambling. What did I expect her to do? Make a diagnosis over the phone?

"Why don't you wait and see what the neurologist has to say? We have some information about ALS we can send to you. You can call me anytime."

I thanked her, gave her my name and address, and hung up. I felt drained. How many calls like this must she get? Of course, she was right. No point jumping to conclusions.

Wait.

Just wait.

The day before the appointment with Dr. Baxter, Carolyn came home for a visit. Our middle child. After graduating from college she was recruited to teach at a private school: junior-high speech and preschool kindergarten. Not a great combination. Not a great experience. That whole scene left her with a bad taste in her mouth for classroom teaching.

For a while she toyed with the idea of going back to school herself, but getting into a routine of studying, taking tests, writing papers was less than appealing. She went into sales. Something she had been doing since she was sixteen. Something she was good at. Something she liked. Besides she didn't have playground duty, or supervised study, or lesson plans, or a junior-higher walking into class saying, "I forget. What were we supposed to do for class?" or preschoolers running into the classroom yelling, "Miss Ball! Miss Ball! Chad peed on me!" Sales were definitely more rational. You did the job, you came home after work, you were done, you had a life.

It worried us. This brightest of children seemed to flit from job to job. Jobs that didn't require her to use her intelligence, only her persuasive skills. We shouldn't have been surprised. Learning came easy for her. While some of her peers worked long hours for good grades, she would wait until the last minute, put something together with minimal effort, and pull an A. She never had to work hard to get good grades. I mean *good* grades. Honor society grades.

Only once, when she was in junior high, do I recall a teacher saying, "She's very bright, you know. Right now she's only using about a quarter of her brain. If Carolyn, would put a little effort into her studies she could turn out some truly remarkable work." What do you say to a child who gets A's without trying? Work harder and get an A?

If we confronted her about her goals, or lack of them, she snapped at us. We backed off. If we nagged or badgered, she got defensive. We had tried everything. All the insights I had acquired about counseling seemed to fly out the window when I was talking with my own daughter.

When the personal computer catapulted into the marketplace,

Bob was hooked. A lover of electronic gadgets, he quickly converted the workplace to computers and taught himself to become computer literate. He frequently opined, "If only Carolyn would get interested in computers. She's always been good at figuring things out. I know she'd love the challenge."

As the computer became more compact, more affordable, it became standard in most businesses and a "must have" at home. Bob tried to steer Carolyn in that direction, but she showed little interest. Like mother, like daughter: *if parents approve, I don't want anything to do with it!*

Finally, we let go. We prayed, "Lord, you care about her more than we do. She's in Your hands, Your child. Help us to encourage her, to enjoy her just the way she is." It's easy to say the words, harder to believe them, harder yet to act on them. At last we got out of the way.

And then, in her own time, she discovered computers. It was like watching a flower blossom. Carolyn and Macintosh. It was a marriage made in megabytes. After a few years selling computers for an office supply company, she started her own consulting and training company. She loved what she was doing. She was good at it. Now she was coming home as a first-time entrepreneur.

As we were getting ready to meet her plane, Bob turned to me and put his hands on my shoulders. He looked at me with those awesome blue eyes, still captivating after all these years, "Remember, this is between us. I really don't want the kids to know there may be a potential problem. No point in getting them all concerned. Okay?"

I nodded. Tomorrow he would see Dr. Baxter during work hours and we'd talk about it when we were alone.

We headed for the airport.

◆ ◆ ◆

I leaned forward to look through the airplane's small window. All I could see were great brown hills. They rose from the basin, barren and dry. I stared in disbelief. This wasn't what I had expected. I had never seen anything like this. Where were the tall evergreens, the lush greenery, the hallmarks of the Pacific Northwest I had heard so much about? The doubts began to form in my mind. Oh, not about Bob, I was more than ready to spend the rest of my life with him, but about this place. At least from the air, it looked like something God forgot. What was I doing here? What was Bob doing here?

Bob had been on campus less than a week when someone in the radio department heard his voice and suggested he try out for the campus station. The voice was impressive; the diction straight out of "Joisey." The engineer running the board for Bob's audition handed him a script and told him to read into the microphone. On cue Bob began, "Kolumbia wrekards presents 'Masterwoiks a' Musick.'" (Translation: Columbia records presents "Masterworks of Music.")

When he glanced up to see how he was doing, the engineer was gone. As Bob stood to see if anyone was there, the engineer, doubled over in laughter, straightened up and waved for Bob to continue. In spite of the accent, Bob got the job and, after speech classes, diction classes, and a stint at the NBC Institute of Broadcasting, he lost the "Joisey" accent and graduated with a degree in radio speech.

The Golden Age of Radio was fading in the wake of a newcomer, television, and the doom-and-gloom sayers predicted radio was on the way out. Regardless, Bob was sure it was here to stay. You couldn't watch television while you were driving.

After sending out umpteen résumés, he had only one solid offer: a CBS radio station in Klamath Falls, Oregon.

He talked to his uncle who had started out in radio broad-casting during those electrifying early days. "It's clear across the country. Mom and Dad aren't too pleased with the idea of my being so far away. What do you think?"

Uncle Ed looked at him for a couple of seconds and then said, "The best advice I can give you is that from Horace Greeley, 'Go West, young man, go West.'"

And so he did. He wanted me to come with him.

My father said, "No way." Radio was part of the enter-tainment industry, and Daddy was absolutely not going to let his daughter go clear across the country to marry an en-tertainer! "Suppose things don't work out? How will you get back home?"

Eventually the plan was for Bob to get settled into the town and his job, fly back to New Jersey after Christmas, we'd get married and then fly back to Klamath Falls to-gether.

Well, the best laid plans, et cetera, et cetera. Bob hadn't counted on the loneliness. Oh, everybody was friendly and warm and he loved his job as a DJ. But at the end of the day they all went home to family, and Bob went home to his hotel room. He was miserable. He yearned for "his Bob-bie," as he called me.

My dad was adamant: "No!"

Little by little I wore him down. Finally he went from "definitely no" to "Okay, you can go *if* you get a job teaching *and* Bob gets a raise. At least you'll have one income coming in if things don't work out."

Ouch! What he meant was: In case Bob gets fired we could live on my income. Just a father looking out for his daughter. He thought he was pretty safe setting those pa-rameters. He didn't realize how driven Bob was to have me by his side.

Bob talked with his boss.

He talked with the superintendent of schools.

He pleaded my case (and his).

Within a week I was offered a teaching job and Bob got a raise.

My dad may have been stubborn and unbending, but he was a man of his word. And so, on a humid August morning, Daddy, my stepmother, my sister, and Bob's family stood on the bridge at LaGuardia and watched as I boarded the plane and took off for San Francisco. All of them had mixed emotions: overjoyed that their offspring were getting married, apprehensive that they would be a continent away.

In the mid-fifties flying was a big deal. I had never flown before. There I was, dressed to the nines: suit by Handmacher, stockings and high heels, hat and white gloves. By the time we landed at Klamath Falls, my feet were swollen, my hair was tangled, and my suit looked as if it had been wadded up on the closet floor for six months. Disheveled but determined, I walked out the door of the plane and scanned the group waiting below. There he was, skinnier than I remembered, holding a bouquet of flowers, smiling and waving. I climbed down the stairs and walked into his arms. We had each other and that's about all.

The next day we were married in the church parsonage. A quiet ceremony—no wedding gown, no tuxedo, no wedding music, just the church pastor with the manager of the radio station and his wife as witnesses.

◆　◆　◆

Bob always regretted that we did not have a formal wedding ceremony but, in the eyes of God, big wedding or wed in front of a fireplace, the vows we said that day satisfied the covenant of marriage.

For better or worse, in sickness and in health, we were one 'til death do us part.

As we waited at the airport for Carolyn's flight to arrive, I commented, "It doesn't seem possible it was more than thirty years ago when you stood at another airport waiting for me. Now we're waiting for Carolyn, all grown up."

He shook his head, "Life's a vapor."

"I love you more today."

He put his arm around me. Just then we saw Carolyn coming through the crowd.

"Do you want me to go to the appointment with you tomorrow?"

"Goodness, no. Just enjoy your time with Carrie."

CHAPTER 4

$\mathscr{A}$s the doctor rushed into the examining room where Bob waited, he yelled over his shoulder, "If Ed calls, put him through!" Then, looking at Bob, he continued, "Honestly, when you want your @%# broker, where is he? Out playing golf, for @%# sake!"

With that startling entrance, Bob met Dr. Baxter.

Dr. Baxter was short.

And fat.

Well, pudgy.

Oh, that's not fair. But he probably never met a food he didn't like.

Slightly balding, late forties, somewhat arrogant—forget somewhat—he was arrogant. He peered at you over his half-glasses. He grunted absently when you tried to describe your symptoms. He interrupted the examination to take a call and talked loudly with his stockbroker or another colleague. You felt as if you were keeping him from something eminently more important.

In spite of all this, he had been highly recommended, and what did we know about medicine or neurology? Frankly, when it came to matters of health, we relinquished control to the specialists. We settled in for the long haul, with Dr. Baxter in charge.

A position he assumed he already had.

"Dr. Hedstrom has referred you for a nerve conduction study. Tell me what's going on, what symptoms are you having?"

Bob sat on the edge of the examination table and related the symptoms he had experienced for the past seven weeks. His left hand was somewhat improved in strength although the twitches (fasciculations) were still present. In retrospect, it is highly probable other muscles were taking over for the dying ones and thus giving the impression of some improvement.

"What got me concerned," Bob went on, "was when I saw a news story about a woman with the same symptoms who was subsequently diagnosed with ALS."

Baxter continued with the examination, asking questions from time to time, checking on the blood work done by Dr. Hedstrom's office, and looking over the medical history Bob completed in the waiting room. He pounced on three things.

Dr. Baxter: "When did you have undulant fever?"

Bob: "Oh, probably around three or four."

Dr. Baxter: "Do you know what caused it?"

Bob: "I remember being told it was from drinking raw milk."

Dr. Baxter: "When did you have mononucleosis?"

Bob: "During college."

Dr. Baxter: "How bad was it? Did you have to drop out of school?"

Bob: "No. I came down with it in the summer. I was really sick. A very bad case. Swollen lymph nodes, spleen so enlarged the doctor feared it might rupture. Miserable time. The doctor wasn't going to let me go back to school if I had to live in the dorm, so I arranged to stay in a small trailer on campus. Actually, that part was kind of neat."

Dr. Baxter: "Your Aunt had Parkinson's?"

Bob nodded.

Dr. Baxter: "Hmmmm."

After more questions and additional prodding and poking, Dr.

Baxter said, "There's a possibility of peripheral neuropathy, which would explain the weakness in your left hand. We often see cases of carpal tunnel syndrome with similar symptoms. We'll do a nerve conduction study to measure the time between nerve stimulation and response, and an electromyogram to measure the electrical activity of the muscles."

"Just the left arm?"

"That's where the symptoms are. It may be a little uncomfortable, but it will only be for a short period of time."

It was uncomfortable, and from time to time Bob would grunt, indicating it was painful. Dr. Baxter would respond, "Just a little longer." Other than that there was little comment. When the testing was completed, the doctor told Bob to put his shirt back on and he'd be back in a few minutes with the results.

When Dr. Baxter returned to the examining room he leaned against the counter, arms folded across his ample belly, and peered at Bob over his half-glasses. "What we have here is puzzling. There is no doubt about the fasciculations, but there is no evidence of widespread denervation."

"What does that mean?"

Baxter gestured with his hands. "The muscles move by the nerve impulses they receive. In spite of the fasciculations you feel in your arm, the muscles are still being stimulated."

"So why am I experiencing weakness in the hand?" Bob questioned.

"There may be local pathology, a localized disease or disorder such as carpal tunnel, which has nothing to do with whatever is causing the fasciculations, those twitchings you are feeling in your arm."

"What about ALS?"

"There is no evidence you have ALS, and there is no reason for you to concern yourself with that possibility. I'll send the results of the test back to Dr. Hedstrom, and I'd like to see you again in about a month. Check at the desk on your way out and Jennifer will make an appointment for your next office visit."

With that he turned on his heels and was out the door.

Bob sat on the edge of the table and blinked. Not quite the conclusion he'd expected. He left the office feeling unsatisfied. As he started to walk out the door, he remembered about the appointment. Turning back, he went to the desk to set up another appointment.

Choosing his words carefully, he asked, "Is he always that, uh, harried?"

The receptionist raised one eyebrow and shook her head from side-to-side. With a small smirk she murmured, "Not much of a bedside manner," as she handed Bob a business card with the date and time of his next appointment.

In his notes, Dr. Baxter wrote of that first meeting, "The results were unexpected. There is no doubt of widespread fasciculations in the left upper extremity, also during the examination patient appeared to have fasciculations throughout his body—including his face. There is no evidence of denervation. However, left hand muscles supplied by C8 and D1 nerves exhibited slight denervation. Patient unduly concerned about ALS. Reassured him the prospect of ALS is highly unlikely."

It was late before we said goodnight to Carolyn and headed off to bed. In the privacy of our bedroom Bob was finally able to talk about the events of the day. I snuggled contentedly next to him as we lay in bed—one of the comfortable perks of years of marriage. He quietly related what had occurred in Dr. Baxter's office.

"So, he doesn't think it's ALS?" I asked when he finished.

"No, it's probably a neuropathy, or carpal tunnel, or something else. I've got another appointment in about a month. You know, this has been a good wakeup call."

"How's that?" I asked.

"Let's put things in perspective. We've got a great marriage, three super kids who have given us very few worries over the years, and now we're starting to reap the blessing of grandkids. I love being a grandpa! It's a wonderful time of life. The only thing that could make it better is if a knight in shining armor would whisk Carrie away. She's got a lot to offer. Don't think I ever told you, when I conjure up a picture of her as a child, she's wearing a lime-green dress and playing the clarinet. I know she played the clarinet, but did she ever have a dress that color?"

"Oh, my goodness. What a memory! She did. I think she was about eleven. She loved that dress. It was a favorite." I don't think he heard me. His steady breathing signaled sleep had overtaken him. But now I was wide awake and thinking about Carolyn.

◆ ◆ ◆

If the weather was nice, Carolyn usually walked home from school lugging her clarinet, hoping to get in a few licks before dinner. In the springtime she would often cut through the wooded lot she passed on the way and bring me a bouquet of trilliums. Most days she got home before I did, but on this day she was late and I was early. She arrived in a state. Not angry, not silly, sort of rattled. At ten years old, almost eleven, she was sometimes temperamental, sometimes moody, but this was different. She fled upstairs without stopping in the kitchen for a snack. I waited patiently for her to come back down.

The old Cape Cod we lived in was of pre-World War II vintage and as solid as the proverbial rock. When we had the basement remodeled into an all-purpose room, the contractor complained that the place was built like a fortress and it took him twice as long as planned to demolish the existing structure. The doors were so tight you couldn't hear a thing in the next room.

Now, I strained to listen for Carolyn. I heard nothing. After a reasonable amount of time, I climbed the stairs to find out what was going on. She was in her bedroom.

"Hey, Sweetie. You comin' down for a snack?"

"Oh, yeah."

As she walked towards the bedroom door, I asked, "Is everything okay?"

She stopped in the doorway. I could see the struggle on her face as to whether or not she should unburden herself. Finally she blurted out, "We saw a cartoon-like movie in class today, well, the girls saw it. It was sort of weird."

"How's that?"

Carolyn looked at the ceiling, at the doorframe, at the floor. I had never seen her so flustered. "It was about babies." She wrinkled up her nose. "How they get here." She proceeded to tell me about the mechanics of reproduction. By the time she finished her face was red and it was obvious she desperately wanted me to contradict her. "That's not right, is it?"

I tried hard not to smile. When you're still at the age where boys are made of "nails and snails and puppy dog's tails," it does sound revolting. But I had to give her an honest answer. "It is."

"Oh." Trying to fathom this new revelation, she asked, "You mean just kind of rolling around in bed it happens?"

"Something like that."

"Did you and Daddy ever do that?"

Oops! I hadn't expected that one. "Well," I gestured towards her with both hands. "Here you are," I replied as evenly as possible.

As she mulled that over it suddenly occurred to her that

she had a brother and a sister. With a look of wide-eyed horror, she exclaimed, "You mean you did it three times!"

Oh, Child-of-love. Someday when Mr. Right comes along you'll understand all these mysteries! With a gentle smile I said, "I suppose we did. That's why we have all three of you. That's why it's important to marry someone you love, someone who loves you in return, so you can provide a loving home for those little babies." I gave her a reassuring hug. "Like we do. Now, how 'bout that snack?"

She seemed satisfied for the moment as arm-in-arm we headed for the kitchen.

◆　◆　◆

I listened to Bob's slow steady breathing. He had always been able to fall off to sleep quickly—a deep, untroubled sleep. If he was untroubled, why was the specter of Lou Gehrig's still racing through my head? I stared into the darkness. Thoughts of Carolyn; thoughts of her daddy. *Lord, I love them both.*

Dr. Baxter walked into the examining room. Without a flicker of recognition he asked, "What brings you here today, Mr. Ball?" Perhaps it was an effort to see if the symptoms remained unchanged. Perhaps he had forgotten he had spent time with Bob less than a month ago. Perhaps he hadn't bothered to look in the folder on his clipboard. More likely he now looked on Bob as his patient, not just a referral from Dr. Hedstrom. Once again Bob told about the apparent sudden onset of weakness in his left hand accompanied by muscular twitching and his concerns about the possibility of ALS.

"Has there been any change since you were last in?" Ah, he did remember.

"Things may have improved a little. At least they appear to be stable."

"Have you muscle weakness anywhere else?"

"Not that I'm aware of."

"The upper arm is okay?"

"Only the pincer grasp is weak."

Even as he extended his forearm outward, the fasciculations in the arm were obvious. Dr. Baxter noted their presence but made no comment. He also observed a slight indentation between the index finger and thumb—a visible sign of muscle wasting. He did not comment on that either. After running Bob through many of the same tests done at the previous visit, he asked, "Have you ever had an MRI?"

The very thought of an MRI filled Bob with terror. He was exceedingly claustrophobic. When he went to bed at night, the window had to be open and there was always a fan running for circulation. If he was on a business trip and the windows in the hotel did not open or the fan in the ventilation system could not be turned on, he always requested a portable fan from housekeeping.

Once we had arrived late in the evening at an older hotel in Washington, D.C. Housekeeping was closed. The windows in the room did not open, and the circulating fan had been shut off for the winter.

"I can't sleep in here!"

"We've been traveling all day. I know you're tired. Let's give it a try."

We closed the drapes, got ready for bed and turned off the lights. In less than a minute he switched on the light. "I'm smothering. I can't breath! There's no air in here!" He sat bolt upright in the bed, threw the covers back, struggled out, and opened the drapes.

"What am I going to do? I've got meetings in the morning." He turned on the TV and watched infomercials, hoping the non-plot programming would bore him to sleep. He paced most of the night like a caged animal.

Now, just thinking about an MRI, his heart rate quickened as he replied in the negative.

"Okay. We'll set you up for an MRI, and, depending on the results, we'll schedule you for a spinal tap."

"Whoa! Wait a minute. First of all, the MRI. I tend to be very claustrophobic. Is it really necessary?"

"If we're going to get answers we have to evaluate the source of the potential problem. It's not an invasive procedure and any abnormalities in the brain stem or upper spine will show up. If you find the procedure too threatening, there is medication you can take that will calm you down and help you get through it. We haven't lost a patient yet, and we're not going to start with you." Baxter grinned condescendingly.

"Do I have to go to the hospital for it?"

"No. There's a clinic that does all of our radiology."

"How about the spinal tap?" Bob asked.

"We do that here in the office. You might want to bring your wife with you. You may not feel like driving home."

Dr. Baxter once again reassured Bob he did not have ALS and he should "get on with his life." In his notes, however, he wrote, "I think that a basically chronic and generalized condition such as ALS must be considered highly unlikely although it perhaps **cannot be entirely excluded**" (emphasis mine).

CHAPTER 5

*W*e sat in the car outside the imaging clinic. I had insisted on coming with Bob just in case the MRI left him too stressed to drive home.

He turned and looked at me apprehensively. "I can't do this. You know how I get."

"I'm sure they get a lot of people who find this an uncomfortable experience. If it's too bad, they'll probably give you something to calm you down."

"You've had one of these, haven't you?" he asked.

I nodded.

"Was it very bad?"

"It's loud."

"What about being confined in such a small space? Did it bother you?"

I shrugged. "No, but you know that being in a confined space doesn't bother me."

"Oh, I'm sorry I'm such a wimp about this." He grimaced.

"Oh, goodness! Everybody has something that gives them the 'ishees.' If I ever came face to face with a tarantula I'd probably drop dead on the spot!"

"I'll take a couple of tarantulas any day rather than stick my head in that tube!" He continued to sit in the parked car. Finally he said, "I'm not goin' in."

"Oh, Honey! I'll be right there with you. Come on."

Reluctantly he got out of the car. I held his arm as we entered the small building. New place, new patient, new forms to complete, including a disclaimer in case of injury or death. That didn't help his mindset.

"I'm getting out of here!" He had no sooner uttered the words then a nurse appeared in the doorway. "Mr. Ball?"

"Want me to come?" I whispered to him.

Bob shook his head and followed the nurse through the door. I stared after him as he disappeared behind the door. I settled into a chair with a three-month-old copy of *Newsweek*. I was still looking through the table of contents when a voice said, "Let's go." It was Bob.

"Are you done already?"

He hustled me out the door before replying, "Couldn't do it. I've got some happy pills, and they've rescheduled me for two weeks from now when we're back from vacation."

The next day we left for Sunriver.

When the first shadow of Lou Gehrig's crossed our path, we wanted to see the children and grandchildren, not to tell them what was wrong since we still weren't sure of the diagnosis, but to spend some time with them. Carolyn had come home for a visit and was now back in South Carolina. Daughter Margie along with her husband, Steve, and their three boys would drive over from Portland and meet us at Sunriver. Son David, wife Cyndi and wee Catherine would join us the next day.

Visibly, the signs of ALS were not apparent. Except for the loss of strength in Bob's left thumb and index finger, his left hand functioned normally. Throughout the time we spent on vacation, he drove the car, went swimming, took hundreds of pictures, went biking on the miles and miles of bike paths, laughed and played with the grandchildren, and walked, and walked, and walked. One brief incident momentarily reminded us of the potential upheaval ahead.

We were all in the multi-purpose room preparing lunch. I handed Bob a jar of pickles, expecting him to open them. He tried for several seconds without success and then handed the jar to David.

"Would you open this?"

David looked at him with a playful smile and quipped, "What's the matter, Bob? Losing muscle strength as you get older?"

Everyone laughed. Our eyes locked briefly across the room as the family bantering continued around us.

This time I was driving. Bob sat docilely beside me. I pulled into the parking lot a little after four.

"You okay?" I asked.

"I am feeling so great. Let's do something after this is over. Let's run away together and not tell your husband!"

He leaned across the seat and gave me a big smooch on the cheek. He was higher than the palm trees surrounding us. We walked into the small office and, with a smile on his face, he readily followed the nurse through the door. I waited anxiously. When five minutes went by without his return, I settled down with a magazine. In about thirty minutes he reappeared with a big grin on his face.

"Done?" I looked up at him.

"Piece of cake! Let's go get a steak. I'm starved."

I couldn't help but love this wacky man. Considering the stress of the past few months, it was like having my sweetheart back again. I hadn't seen him this euphoric since David was born. "Let's." I grinned back at him as I clutched his arm.

◆　◆　◆

With each pregnancy I had gained more weight. The doctor wasn't concerned since I seemed to lose it quickly once the baby was born. Now, near the end of this third pregnancy, I was huge. I had added fifty pounds to my small frame. I was sick of eating cottage cheese and tomatoes, drinking blue milk, and waddling. It had been so long since I could see my feet I just had to trust Bob when he said they were still there.

After producing two girls, we were pretty sure it was going to be another girl. We even had a girl's name picked out: Pamela Joy.

"Don't you think we ought to have a boy's name ready just in case?" I asked.

"Oh, I suppose," he answered without much conviction. "How about Robert Wilson Ball III?"

"I love my Dad, but I really hate my middle name. I guess we could call him Robert." He sounded less than enthusiastic. We were interrupted by one of the girls, and the subject was dropped.

Days before my due date, Bob's mom and dad flew in from New Jersey, hoping the timing would be right to be with our little family when their third grandchild was born. Sure enough, a few days after they arrived we left for the hospital.

With our first child, I was hustled away as soon as we walked into the hospital. Bob was ushered into the waiting room, where he waited, and waited, and waited, all the while thinking worst-case scenario and praying fiercely. In just four years things had progressed to where he was now allowed to stay with me during labor, but still shooed out of the room when delivery was imminent. Once again he found himself in the dreaded waiting room.

He stood up when the nurse entered.

"Mr. Ball?"

He nodded.

"You have a nice, healthy boy."

He stared at her for a few seconds and then sat back down. "Are you sure?" he asked, continuing to stare at her. "Trust me." She smiled. "I've seen lots."

He wasn't prepared for the wave of elation that swept over him. He was positively giddy. He floated down the hospital corridor to the nursery and stood there mesmerized looking at his infant son. When the nurse finally placed the swaddled baby in his arms, he asked again, "Are you sure it's a boy?"

He called his folks, who were looking after the girls at home. When his father answered, he blurted out, "Congratulations! You're grandparents again! Tell the girls I'll be home soon." With that he hung up.

Grandma looked at Grandpa as he stood holding the phone in his hands. "Well? Did they have the baby?"

"Yes."

"What is it?"

"I have no idea!"

When he was finally allowed to see me, he looked at me lovingly then tenderly kissed me on the cheek. "You gave me a boy. He's beautiful," he said softly. "I think I'll keep you."

Eventually he came down to earth and decided that Pamela Joy wouldn't be a suitable name for his son. We decided on David, "beloved of God," beloved of his father.

♦   ♦   ♦

The rush from the "happy pills" wore off and, now, a week later, Bob sat on the edge of the examining table in Baxter's office wearing the usual designer gown. We were waiting for the spinal tap.

I searched his face. "You uneasy?"

"A little," he replied. "I suppose it's like anything you do for the first time. You're not sure what to expect, so you get a bit apprehensive."

Dr. Baxter walked in and, after a cursory physical exam, had Bob lie on the table in a fetal position. "It's important that you lie very still during this procedure. It won't take long." After shooting a little lidocaine into the space between vertebrae L4-L5, he attempted to insert a needle.

"Oops!" he muttered. Now, of all the things you want to hear uttered by your physician, "oops" is not one of them. Especially when it involves the spinal cord. Bob glanced at me helplessly.

"Problem?" I asked, trying not to let the concern show in my voice.

"No. Just encountered some bony resistance. I'll reposition between L3-L4."

As he tried again, a stifled groan escaped from Bob's mouth.

"Just a little longer Mr. Ball. I'm withdrawing fluid right now. It's almost over."

When Dr. Baxter was done, he left the room, after cautioning Bob to remain in a supine position. We waited.

About thirty minutes later Dr. Baxter returned. Looking at Bob, he said, "Well, the fluid I just withdrew appears to be normal. To the naked eye it was clear and colorless, but it will go to the lab for routine and microbiological analysis. All of the lab work we've done to this point has been normal. All the results have been benign. No lesions. Call me in about two days for the results of the spinal fluid and then I'd like to see you in about ten days for follow-up."

I looked at the doctor. "Dr. Baxter, it's becoming more difficult to make plans when we don't have a specific diagnosis. What about the possibility of ALS? Should we be exploring that?"

For a moment Dr. Baxter's nostrils flared. *Uh-oh, I dared to question his eminence.* When he spoke his words were clipped. "We're running all the tests necessary in an attempt to find the problem. There is no evidence he has ALS. I suggest you get on with your life and live as you normally would."

With that he walked out of the room. I wrinkled my nose as I looked at Bob. "Well, I guess I've been told!"

By the calendar, it was almost five months since the first manifestation of muscle weakness and recurrent twitches. We had openly and often discussed the possibility of a serious diagnosis. Early on Bob considered getting more life insurance (all he had was $75,000, a large sum when we first married, but a mere pittance now). In characteristic integrity, he decided it wouldn't be honest, even though no one had made a diagnosis.

He toyed with the idea of moving back to Oregon, even suggesting I look for work there.

"Why would you want me to do that?"

"If no one is around to see me losing, uh, getting weaker you know I do most of my work over the telephone. With a fax machine and the telephone I could really work from anywhere."

"You mean you want to move back to Oregon?"

"It might not be a bad idea. If you got a job it would make more sense to move. Besides, you could add to your retirement fund. You know I don't have any pension plan like Dad did, and the money in the IRA, well, that's a laugh."

"You really want me to check it out?"

"I do."

The next day I checked the listings. A suburban district in Oregon was seeking a school psychologist. I faxed my résumé. A few days later, the director of special services called and, after we talked for a while, asked if I'd be willing to fly up for an interview. I agreed and told him I'd phone with the details.

That evening after dinner I said, "I got a call today from Oregon. They want me to fly up for an interview."

"No kidding! That's great!"

I put my hand on his arm, not to feel the ever-present twitches, which I did, but to make sure I had his attention. "Bob, do you really want to do this? Do you want to move? Do you want me to go back to work? If you're sure this is what you want, I'll do it in a heartbeat. You know I love working with children. I'll book a flight tomorrow morning, but only if you're sure you want to do this. I can't string these people along."

He looked down at his empty plate and absently toyed with the silverware. When he finally spoke, it was barely audible. "It seemed like a good idea at the time. It's one thing for Baxter to say 'just get on with your life,' it's another thing when you have long-range decisions to make. This not knowing for sure whether or not we're dealing with a terminal disease is almost paralyzing. I guess I'm just selfish, but if it is what we think I don't want anyone else taking care of me except you. I guess that means I don't really want you going back to work. I don't think I can go through ALS without you by my side."

His eyes were awash with tears when he finished.

"Honey, you're not being selfish. If I can't see you through the dark times as well as the mountaintops, then our marriage vows were hollow."

It was settled. The door was shut. The subject was never mentioned again. But in truth we were in flux.

That night Bob called Sam Costene, a neurosurgeon. He and Sam had met years earlier and, even though they lived thousands of miles apart, developed a mutual respect for each other's proficiency. Now Bob was hoping for a little input from this man who would, without question, honor the confidentiality of the situation. After exchanging pleasantries, Bob shared the events of the past five months.

When he finished, there was a rather long silence, then Dr.

Costene said, "Well, they have certainly been checking you out. It could be a lot of things. Look, if I can be of any help, get you a referral to USC, or Mayo, or Henry Ford, just call. They're all on the cutting edge of neurological diseases."

They talked for a little longer. After hanging up, Bob sat there quietly.

"What did Sam say?"

"He said, 'Let's hope it's not one of the baddies.'"

We were learning what ALS victims the world over already knew. Doctors do not want to make this diagnosis. The physician has been trained to cure, to heal. He is ill-prepared to say "there is nothing we can do" and send the patient home to die.

In defense of the medical profession, there is no one test to confirm the presence of ALS. The patient must go through test after test to rule out other neurological conditions. However, even when the tests come back negative, the patient is often subjected to them again and again in the hope of finding some treatable condition.

As we entered month six we still had no answers. Bob continued to see Dr. Baxter. The strength in his left hand fluctuated from almost normal one day to practically useless the next. The fasciculations persisted in his hand and arm and, from time-to-time, could be seen in other parts of his body. When he continued to express concern about the possibility of ALS, Dr. Baxter once again reassured him there was no evidence of such a grim outlook. In his notes he remarked: "Patient reassurance. Even so, he is becoming more difficult, due to continued anxiety regarding a serious diagnosis."

Dr. Baxter scheduled another MRI, this one of the brain, and further EMG (electromyography) to measure electrical activity of the muscles. The MRI results were normal. The EMG abnormal. All four limbs were subjected to the EMG testing, but only results from the left arm were abnormal. Dr. Baxter's analysis was that the

EMG results supported localized pathology of the left arm and not a generalized motor neuron disease such as ALS. He told Bob to get his life back on the main track.

And so we tried. In October (month eight) we went on a cruise—a much-needed break from work and health problems. We went with a group of fellow broadcasters we had known for years. We sailed the Caribbean with lots of friends and lots of good food. It was wonderful. We soaked up the sun, signed up for all the tours, went snorkeling, took plenty of pictures, and ate ourselves into Weight Watchers.

The tour route took us to St. Thomas. We had been there before and were still amazed at how much the center of this tropical paradise resembled Manhattan's 42nd Street. Shops, shops, shops, all selling trinkets to the hordes of tourists spewed out by the cruise ships.

This time we slipped away to the back streets, searching for a small synagogue highlighted on the map. As we entered the building, two women spoke in hushed tones relating the history of this house of worship. The sanctuary was established in 1796 and destroyed twice by fire. The present structure was erected in 1833. The women in the lobby offered Bob a yarmulke (skullcap), and we walked quietly into the sanctuary through heavy double doors. It was lovely, an oasis of calm amid all the activity. We sat in a mahogany pew. In the quiet of the moment he reached over and held my hand tightly. I don't know what thoughts were going through his mind, but the words of King Solomon exploded in mine:

"In the day of prosperity, be joyful;

But, in the day of adversity consider,

God has made the one as well as the other." (Ecclesiastes 7:14)

The last phrase seemed to echo through my head. Our meditative silence was broken by a noisy, laughing group entering the building. We left.

One afternoon at lunch or teatime or some other gastronomical event (there was always food), I arrived late, and the only seat left at the table was across from Bob. As I settled into the empty chair, the young man on my right asked, "Are you right-handed?"

"Yes."

"Aw-oh. I'm left-handed. I usually try to sit beside another left-handed person. You may get elbowed. It's nothing personal," he said with a laugh.

"Oh, I'm used to lefties. Bob's…" my voice trailed off. As I said his name, I glanced over at him. He was eating with his right hand. Fortunately the chatter around the table covered any lapse in the conversation. It was another out-of-body experience. I ate, but I was caught up in my own thoughts. *How long had this been going on? How could I not have noticed? Had we been married for so long that I just assumed the status quo?* As I browbeat myself for being unobservant, I silently prayed, *Lord, make me more observant. He needs me now more than ever.*

Back in the cabin, I asked, "How long have you been using your right hand for eating?"

"Oh, off and on. Depends on the strength in the fingers."

"Is there anything else you're having trouble with?"

His response was slow in coming. "Buttons," he said.

A bucket of ice water sloshed over me. In the millisecond following that one word, the definition I had read months earlier flashed through my mind: "difficulty with the tasks of daily living, such as buttoning clothes."

I stretched my arms up around his neck and, with a lightness I did not feel, said, "You know, if you need help with buttons or anything, just whistle. 'You know how to whistle, don't you?'" I smiled as I touched his lips. For the rest of the cruise I didn't let him out of my sight.

Out here, surrounded by miles and miles of sparkling blue water, an elephant lounged by the ship's pool.

CHAPTER 6

$\mathcal{W}$e were back home unpacking, adjusting to life on terra firma, and bit-by-bit coming down from the high of cruising. As we hung up clothes and sorted through treasures, I uncovered the packet of photographs taken by the staff and handed to us at the end of the journey. Opening the folder, I spread the pictures out on the bed. Bob hovered beside me as I knelt by the bed to scrutinize the images. Glancing over the array of photos, I remarked, "I really like this one," pointing to the two of us standing side by side.

"I don't."

Startled by the tone of his voice, I looked up. "Why not?"

"It shows the muscle wasting in my left hand."

I picked up the picture. We stood close together. His right arm was wrapped around me with a firm grip on my arm. His left arm hung at his side. Between the thumb and index finger of his left hand there was a depression. Not a small indentation. A large, concave hollow big enough to hold a golf ball. I stared at it.

Strike two!

For years I had been employed as a school psychologist. We were trained to observe everything. The moment the child came into the room, you watched, like a hawk. His gait, the way he held his pencil and positioned his paper, which hand he used, his posture when sitting, how he held his head, whether he squinted. You watched for overflow movements or the constant small movement that looked like water simmering on the stove. You listened for speech abnormalities or lack of the same. By the time you spent fifteen minutes with the child, you probably knew him better than his teacher.

So, what was wrong here? Why wasn't I catching these in-your-face signals? Was it because I looked at Bob through eyes of love and acceptance instead of the critical view of an objective observer?

My eyes filled with tears. I managed to keep them from spilling over. "Honey, we have to find out what's wrong."

His answer was soft and tinged with weariness, "We already *know* what's wrong. Nobody seems willing to even consider the possibility of ALS."

Outwardly, Bob looked great. Healthy as a horse. His blood pressure hovered around 124/78; his cholesterol level an astonishing 165. For someone who loved thick, rare steaks, butter, and salt, those readings defied all medical admonitions. There was no evidence of any abnormality—until you looked closer.

The fasciculations continued to race through his arm. The weakness in his left thumb and index finger was more pronounced. The strength in his left hand was diminishing. In spite of all the visible signs, by relying heavily on his right hand, he was able to carry a briefcase, open a door, drive a car. The muscles throughout the upper left arm appeared unaffected despite the ever-present twitches.

About this time there was a change in Baxter's reporting. Up to now the comments of each visit had been typed, taking up a page or more of single-spaced text. But from the seventh month under his care until we terminated the relationship after fifteen months of strain, the report of each visit was handwritten on one-third sheet of paper. Had he given up? Although Bob still went through frequent checkups and multiple tests, Baxter's attitude became more detached. In his hand-written notes for October, he concluded, "proposing to send him to Mayo for additional opinion." He never did. He never even discussed this possibility with Bob.

The next appointment was in early December, month ten.

Bob told the doctor, "I seem to be getting worse. Bobbie and I have tried to keep this between us until we had some answers. If I have ALS, it's not ethical for me to keep that information from my employer or the people who depend on me."

"Mr. Ball, your symptoms are very, very focal. Not indicative of a pervasive disease."

Even as he spoke Dr. Baxter observed fasciculations in the right arm and both legs, but the only limb evidencing obvious weakness was still the left arm. Not willing or able to admit he was stymied by the diagnostic information or lack of it, he kept searching for the smallest indication this was a treatable condition.

After running Bob through the usual tests, he suggested some hand and arm exercises.

"Like what?"

"Oh, keep a nerf ball handy or silly putty, something of that nature. Squeeze it when you're on the phone or watching television."

"How about a hand grip?" (He was already using one.)

"Couldn't hurt. It's been almost six months since you had the cervical MRI. Let's schedule another one to determine if there has been any change. My receptionist will set it up for you." With that he was gone. Another MRI. Number three.

The next day we flew to New York City. The parent company had acquired a radio station in New York, and Bob was anxious to see the operation and encourage the staff. One problem. He could no longer manage those tiny shirt buttons. Large buttons, like those on a suit or overcoat, were manageable with the fingers of his right hand and minimal left-handed assistance, but each morning I buttoned his shirt.

It was obvious: I had to go with him. The question, how could he include me without raising a lot of curiosity as to why I was suddenly going with him on a business trip. Since I had lived in Manhattan for a couple of years, that became the perfect excuse for me to go along. Just to visit the old haunts. At our own expense, my name was added to the itinerary.

We checked into a hotel in midtown Manhattan. Our room was big enough for one bed, one chair, one dresser, and a cockroach the size of a Cadillac doing pushups in the corner. If you saw one, you knew there were more. For years I'd surmised that the buildings in the city were reinforced by cockroaches. If the roaches were to get wiped out by some cockroachean plague, the bulk of Manhattan would collapse.

The next morning I helped Bob get ready for the day. He assured me he'd be fine.

"What about lunch?" I asked him. "Will you be okay?"

"Oh, yes. I just won't order anything too big. Probably a corned beef sandwich or pastrami. New York's got the best." He smiled, kissed me, and was gone.

The room smelled of stale smoke and decades of use. Not wanting to spend the day in such a depressing environment or in the company of resident roaches, I left.

For all the tearing down and building up again, things were pretty much the same. I set out on foot with no destination in mind, just enjoying the sunny December day and the personality of the city. Eventually my steps led me past Calvary Baptist Church on West 57th. I stopped and stared at the familiar structure. For a moment I was young again, holding my father's hand, walking up the stairs and through the massive doors. Vivid memories from childhood drew me inside.

◆ ◆ ◆

I woke with a start. The wail of sirens echoed through the city canyons and exploded into the bedroom. I struggled to make some sense of the sound. Where was I? And then I remembered. My first day in the big city. Welcome. I stuck my head under the pillow and began to cry.

Yesterday we climbed into the Dodge and followed the moving van as it headed slowly towards our new home: New York City. I already hated it. I wanted to be back in my old house, in my old neighborhood, in my old school.

All I knew was life in South Jersey. We lived in Point Pleasant, a small coastal town, overrun with vacationers in the summer months, empty and quiet after Labor Day. The town seemed to let out a collective sigh when the last tourist left and the shops along the boardwalk boarded up against the approaching hurricane season. The town was ours for the next nine months.

It was an idyllic place for a child. Small enough to walk to school; big enough to have its own movie theater, where for nine cents you could buy a ticket for the Saturday matinee.

The main staple of the town was Johnson's Hardware. If Johnson's didn't have it, it probably didn't exist. Filled with everything a homeowner could want: dishes, furniture, toys, appliances, plus all the nuts and bolts of a hardware store. A bell jangled when the door opened and you entered this wonderland for grownups.

It was cool inside and dimly lit. It smelled of furniture polish, floor wax, evergreen, and disinfectant. The hardwood floors creaked beneath your feet. A grand staircase led to the balcony at the rear. As a child, you were sure someone was watching you from that balcony or that it might be filled with a choir of angels. The admonition of "stay close beside me" seldom needed to be said. This was not a place to run around or wander off. This was a place you entered with respect and a trace of reverential awe.

My favorite building in town was the library. Dark and old and filled with books, to me it was the most wonderful place in the world. So many stories to be read. I tended to read one author until the books ran out. Louisa May Alcott, Albert Payson Terhune, Opal Wheeler, Marguerite Henry, Gene Stratton-Porter, Daphne du Maurier and, of course, all the Nancy Drew mysteries. I would beg Mom to leave me there when she went shopping. At least once a week, I would check out an armful of books. I must admit, I coveted all those books.

Living in our little paradise did not come without sacrifice. Daddy worked on Wall Street. His lengthy commute by train morning and evening finally became too much. We leased the house at the shore and moved to Manhattan—to an apartment on the tenth floor.

The school I was assigned to did not even have a proper name, just a number: PS 165. It was huge. A three story brick building opening on an asphalt courtyard that passed for the playground. Not so much as a blade of grass.

My rural school had one room for each grade. No surprises about who your teacher would be. If you were in second grade it was Mrs. Lawrence, if you were in fifth it was Miss Wilcox.

There were so many classrooms at PS 165 you could get lost in the building. I was in sixth grade, but there was 6AR, 6A1, 6A2, 6A3, 6A4, and 6A5. I suppose they didn't know what to do with this skinny, little kid wearing big owl-like eyeglasses and smelling faintly of salty ocean air. They plugged me into 6AR, the rapid division.

It was different. Lily Wang and I were the only goyim (gentiles) in the classroom. On Jewish holidays, and it seemed there was at least one every month, Lily and I had the classroom to ourselves. To keep the entire class on track, actual teaching was suspended on those days and Lily and I spent a lot of time reading library books, drawing pictures, and playing board games. We became close school chums.

I soon learned to travel around the city by myself. You could take the subway anywhere for a nickel. I shudder to think of it now, a ten-year-old girl traveling around Manhattan unaccompanied. Every week I rode the subway to take piano lessons from Madame Sokovski. She would bellow at me if the rhythm was off and stomp about the room yelling, "One, two, three! One, two, three!" I cringed when she shouted that I was a disgrace because I didn't practice enough. After all that, when lessons were over she'd plant a wet kiss on my cheek as I was leaving and tell the next victim waiting in the hall how wonderfully I played. "She's a genius! Such talent! Ve should bottle it and sell it!" Out of earshot we referred to her as "the mad Russian."

Just because you become familiar with a place doesn't mean you like it. I yearned for green grass, the inlet we lived on, the pervasive smell of the sea, the warm sand beneath my feet and between my toes.

Over time, even though I wanted to hate it all, there were things about the city I grew to love. Macy's windows at Christmas were magical. Watching skaters glide over the ice at Rockefeller Center, the Museum of Natural History, the great lions in front of the New York Public Library, the newsreel theaters, the Rockettes, the Yankees, even the Brooklyn Dodgers.

And then there was the food. Even as a child I enjoyed the food. Downright good food. Everywhere. Visits to the automat, with its endless array of food displayed behind shiny glass windows. I dropped a nickel or two, or three, into the slot, and plucked a treasure from the glass cubicle.

So much to choose from. Anything I wanted. At Walgreen's lunch counter I climbed on the revolving stool and ordered a creamy chocolate malt shake with a side of french fries. Made me feel so grown-up. Not a very nutritious lunch, but then I never had enough money to do it often. There were also infrequent visits to Child's Restaurant, with its plate-size pancakes, and the sidewalk hot dog vendor, where I bought my first cup of coffee.

Who could live in New York and ever forget the taste of bagels, kaiser rolls with crunchy crusts and tender insides, and corned beef or pastrami sandwiches, with the meat heaped so high between slices of rye bread you couldn't get your mouth around it? And the cheesecake, heavy and rich. It lingered on your tongue and melted in your mouth. You savored every bite. Even the family-owned Chinese restaurant nearby, hidden away in a second floor walk-up, served a jumbo shrimp in lobster sauce that I still dream about. Beyond delicious.

After two years in the Big Apple, we returned to the little coastal town I thought of as home. The memories of crowds, cacophony, and concrete, concrete, concrete, would dim. The tastes never would.

◆ ◆ ◆

Organ music filled the church. With all the stops pulled out, the music enveloped me as I walked in. It took my breath away. In a heartbeat I became one with the organ as the glorious sounds of "Joy to the World" burst forth in a crescendo of praise for God's great gift to mankind. When the music ceased, a holy hush settled over the sanctuary. After a short pause, the gentle strains of "Jesu, Joy of Man's Desiring" flooded my soul. I edged into a pew in the back and let the music wash over me.

I don't know how long I sat there, but I suddenly realized the music had stopped and I was alone. I walked outside and shivered in the sun of a cold December day.

The New York part of the trip went off without a glitch. Bob felt invigorated and somewhat envious of the young lions eager to succeed in a new venture.

"If I were thirty years younger…" His voice trailed off.

When Bob set up the itinerary, it seemed only logical to include a quick trip up to the company-owned radio station in Boston. On impulse he told his secretary to schedule us on Amtrak for the New York-Boston leg and we would fly back to LA out of Logan airport in Boston. We hailed a cab and headed for Pennsylvania Station.

The center of bustling activity that I remembered as a child held only a handful of people. We picked up our tickets and waited on the platform for the train. Although we had frequently traveled by train as children, we had never traveled together on one. We felt like young kids. An adventure.

"How you doing?" I asked.

"I'm great. I love having you with me." He leaned down and planted a kiss on my cheek.

Standing on the platform, a flickering wave of apprehension began to grow. Traveling by train is different. For one thing, no assigned seats. You hope you can find two together. Another thing, unless you have something really big, like a trunk or a bicycle, you are expected to carry your luggage on board. The passenger cars are outfitted with overhead racks to store your belongings.

We boarded the train and quickly found seats. Bob hoisted the suitcase to put it in the overhead rack. It got close to the rack, but his left arm was not strong enough to complete the maneuver. The suitcase crashed to the seat. Getting a firm grip with his right hand, he tried again. It dropped to the seat. A glint of perspiration appeared on his forehead. He started to lift the heavy suitcase for the third time.

At that moment, a young man bounded from his seat across the aisle. "Here, let me help you with that." He lifted the suitcase as if it were empty and carefully stowed it on the rack.

"Thank you," I said.

"Yeah. Thanks a lot." The strain in Bob's voice was evident.

"No problem."

We moved into the row of seats and sat in silence. Finally, with a look of resignation and a voice lacking expression, he muttered, "I feel really useless."

I didn't know what to say. I reached over and laid my hand on his. He shook it off. The moment of joyful camaraderie between us on the station platform had disappeared.

The elephant in the tea was back.

CHAPTER 7

arkness had settled over the neighborhood by the time we began our walk. Transformed with the glow of Christmas lights and lawn decorations, all it needed was a light sprinkling of snow. *In your dreams.*

Poinsettias grew in the gardens and branches of red bougainvillea cascaded over fences and rooftops. Weird. We still felt off-kilter with the lack of seasonal change in California. It seemed strangely out of sync at Christmas to glimpse people in the mall wearing shorts and tank tops. For the first time since our marriage, I had difficulty mustering up any enthusiasm for Christmas shopping.

"When are you scheduled for the next MRI?" I asked.

"Not until after the first of the year. Why do you ask?"

"I need to put it on the calendar. You'll be taking Valium, so I should probably drive you there. Right?"

"I'm sorry I'm such a bother."

I heard an edge to his voice and turned to look at him. Ever since we'd returned home from Boston last week, Bob seemed to be itching for a fight. "Honey! You're not a bother. I just need to know when your appointment is."

"It's in my computer. I'll let you know."

We continued walking in silence.

CHAPTER 7

The next day it was shirts. I was fixing dinner. Bob, home after a full day of work, was in the bedroom changing into walking clothes. "Barbara!"

I could tell from the sound of his voice something was wrong. I hurried into the bedroom.

He stood in front of the open closet door. "Where are my shirts?"

That afternoon I had stopped at the laundry to pick up his shirts. I looked in the closet. There were six or seven shirts on hangers. Nodding towards the closet, I replied, "They're there."

"No, I had lots more than that."

"I just picked them up today. That's it."

"Well you must not have gotten them all."

"Yes I did. That's all they had."

"I know I had more."

"We had the laundry fold some for packing when we went back to New York. They're probably still in the boxes."

"They're trying to cheat you."

I could hardly believe what I was hearing. My usually logical husband glared into the closet as he spoke. "Bob, they are not!"

"It's that laundry. They're destroying my shirts!" By now he was getting agitated.

"Honey! They're honorable people. They wouldn't do that!"

"Why do you always do that?"

I backed off in surprise. "What?"

"Always take the other side."

"I do not!"

"Yes you do! You never agree with me!"

I was suddenly aware of how ludicrous we sounded. We were arguing over shirts. Shirts! The threat of a terminal illness hovered between us and we were squabbling about laundry? This wasn't about missing shirts. It went far deeper. He was losing control of his world. He had to lash out, to vent his anger on something.

"Oh, Bob." I threw my arms around him. He was rigid. "Don't do this. Please. Let's not argue. I love you so much." I buried my head against his chest and held on. His agitation slowly subsided. As I felt him relax, he put his arms around me and rested his head on top of mine. We clung to each other in silence.

"I'll always be here for you," I murmured, "no matter what."

◆　◆　◆

"Did you have trouble adjusting to married life? I mean, when you first got married was it hard living with someone else?" She looked around the lunch table at all of us.

We were a varied group. Our ages spanned at least thirty years. Our marital status ranged from single to newlywed to widow. We all worked in special services, and even though our chosen fields of service differed, the educational setting had bonded us into a close-knit sisterhood. We were a team.

"Don't ask me," I responded. "We knew each other for so many years before we got married that living together was a breeze. We didn't have any adjustment problems." I shrugged and gestured with my hands. "*Now* we're having problems." Everyone laughed.

But it was true. There was a rift between us, and it was growing wider with each passing day.

Not the usual problems you read about in marriage manuals.

Money? We seldom clashed over money. At the outset, Bob determined to provide for his family and he did. We lived on his salary. Any money I brought in went for extras. Things we didn't need. Things we could live without. Like remodeling the kitchen or building a cabin at the beach or buying a canoe.

Fidelity? Never in question. We meant our vows, and the passion in our marriage was just that, within the marriage. A little less intense than when we first married, but warmer, deeper, more comfortable.

So what was the problem?

For one thing, we reacted to events differently. With Bob the emotional outburst was immediate. It made no difference what the impending situation called for—sorrow, anger, fear—his reaction was swift and then it was over, done, finished, forgotten. He immediately put the incident behind him. Like a fleeting cloudburst, the thunderclouds passed, the sun came out, and all was well.

Not exactly.

I was slow to respond and, like the perpetual drizzle of the Northwest, my reaction lingered for days, sometimes weeks. While Bob was once again "getting on with things," I was stuck in the muck trying to get my emotions in check. He could barely recall the incident while I continued to dwell on it. With a click of the mouse his screen was cleared. My computer kept coming up with the message, "Are you sure you want to delete this?" and I would hit "No."

I considered Bob's capacity to erase the unpleasantness as insensitive, uncaring. He was back to business as usual; I was left with a lingering knot in my stomach. Eventually I accepted his ability to wipe out the negative as part of his persona; it wasn't going to change. To manage, I often punched my own chaotic emotions down inside, and got back to loving and living, and caring for a growing family while the knot subsided.

Our goal from the time the children could stand on their own two feet was to encourage responsible, independent behavior. As they grew more independent, Bob found it increasingly difficult to cope with this surge of autonomy. He was successful and in charge in the business world only to come home and go toe-to-toe with a teenager. At work he was the unquestioned voice of authority. He spoke, someone listened. He gave instructions, they were followed. He expected results, not excuses. At home his authority was questioned. A self-proclaimed "control freak," he coped with the loss of control by retreating to his study or darkroom.

Now, for the first time in twenty-two years, we were alone. The children were gone: Margie teaching in Florida, Carolyn and David off to college. So much of our conversation had centered around the needs and pressures of growing children, we suddenly found ourselves with little to say to each other. As our interaction decreased, I didn't even realize I was building a wall between us. Bob reacted to this isolation by retreating to his darkroom.

When we were together he expressed irritation over things beyond his control: a stoplight that slowed his progress or a driver who dared to cut him off or a slow-moving checkout line. Outbursts over seemingly trivial events. If I called attention to his over-the-top response, he lashed out at me. Each display of anger spilled over and left me feeling remote and defensive, further isolating us from the closeness we had always shared, driving a wedge between us.

Was the marriage itself in jeopardy? No. It was tied with a knot, not a slipknot; but our relationship was strained, almost adversarial.

The laughter was gone.

We were adrift.

We didn't know each other anymore.

We weren't sure we even liked each other anymore.

It was a dreadful time.

Thankfully, it didn't last long.

In a few weeks things came to a head. We had just gotten

CHAPTER 7

into bed when Bob began to talk in quiet, measured tones. "I'm not sure what's going on between us, but you've become cold and distant. You've built a wall between us. You're negative about everything I do. I don't like to come home anymore. Something's got to change. I don't deserve this kind of treatment."

I was stunned. I wanted to lash out with verbal accusations of my own. Didn't he know the reason I was distant was in response to his behavior? That I couldn't deal with his unpredictable outbursts of anger? I was the wounded party. What right did he have to criticize my actions? The words piled up on my tongue and threatened to explode out of my mouth.

Years earlier, during his sometimes challenging teens, David spoke to his father in anger and with more than a little disrespect. As our son stormed out of the room, I confronted him in the small hallway at the bottom of the stairs. We stared at each other. His eyes blazed and his jaw was set.

"David, I love you very much, but I don't like what you just did. You owe your father an apology."

"Well, he made me mad. And he was wrong."

I looked up at this man-child, a head taller and pounds heavier than I. "Right or wrong he's your father. He deserves to be treated with respect. If you can't control your tongue, leave, get out of the room. Better to risk his anger by walking away than stay and say something you'll regret."

Now I heeded my own advice. For once in my life I said nothing. I knew if I spoke the words racing through my head they would hang between us forever. After a few minutes of silence, Bob turned away.

In the darkness I slipped out of bed and went downstairs to the kitchen, so angry I was trembling. I turned on the light, sat at the counter, and opened my Bible. I already

70

knew the Biblical injunctions to husbands and wives, but if I was to love and respect my husband, didn't he need to follow God's commands first? I wanted to find something, anything, that acknowledged my actions depended on Bob fulfilling his responsibility first. Looking in the concordance, I checked every reference having to do with marriage, husband, wife, family. I searched the Scriptures hoping to find something, anything to vindicate my behavior.

That night, as I laid bare my soul before the Spirit of God, I could find no ifs. My actions were not dependent on Bob's behavior. Whether or not he acted the way I thought he should, my responsibility as a wife was clear: I was to love and respect my husband. Period.

If God in His holiness loved Bob just as he was, with an everlasting love, could I do any less? Did I think I was better than God? It was not my job to change Bob or, for that matter, to expect him to change. That was God's job if He chose to do it. My job was to love my husband.

Had the love we shared when we declared our wedding vows been eclipsed by twenty-two years of meeting children's needs? In those early morning hours I knew I loved him more than when we first married. I knew I desperately wanted things to be better. I turned to I Corinthians 13, Paul's inspired litany describing the character of love. The very first description caused me to put my head in my hands: "Love suffers long and is kind." Patient and kind.

I had to confess before God that I was wrong. I prayed that it wasn't too late to bring back that selfless first love. It was almost 3:00 a.m. before I turned off the lights and quietly went back upstairs.

The next morning Bob walked into the kitchen as I readied breakfast. With the memory of last night fresh in his mind, he asked, "Are you okay?"

The first words from Bob's mouth were concern for my well-being. *Oh, thank you, Lord!*

I stopped grinding the coffee. "Honey, I'm sorry. I've behaved very badly towards you. Can you forgive me? Can we start over?"

In a step he was next to me. Without hesitation he wrapped his arms around me and said, "Oh, Bobbie Jean, I know I'm not the easiest person to live with. I've always loved you and always will. I think I'd die if you ever left me. Let's start again."

The fire between us had been reduced to a few embers, but those embers still glowed. We set about fanning the flame back to life. He brought me flowers. I left love notes on his windshield and in the pocket of his suit jacket. He took me out to dinner. I sent him balloons at work. We went for long walks, and talked, and talked, and talked. We were like newlyweds. Crazy in love. We not only loved each other, we *liked* each other. Lovers and best friends. We had almost lost something precious, but, by the grace of God, we found it again. We were one, forever.

◆ ◆ ◆

That rocky hiccup occurred almost twelve years ago. Now our marriage was deeper and fuller than either of us could have imagined. We nurtured the bond on a daily basis. Never again would we take our relationship for granted. Never again would we keep a balance sheet. I loved him with a deep, abiding, God-given love that would carry us through any elephant-in-the-tea event. Even the ravages of ALS.

We approached the new year with some optimism. Maybe we'd get some answers from this new MRI. However, a week later even the Valium didn't seem to lift Bob's spirits as I drove him home from the clinic. "Let's take inventory of what I've had done so far."

"Okay."

"I've had three MRIs, two nerve conduction studies, two EMGs, one neck x-ray, one spinal tap, 'and a partridge in a pear tree.'" He interjected the melody with a smile. "Sorry."

I shook my head. With all the problems, he still had his sense of humor.

"To continue: all kinds of blood work to rule out such things as polio, metal poisoning, virus, rheumatic fever, arthritis, Lyme disease, multiple sclerosis. I've been checked for tumors and cysts, prodded and poked. We've spent an enormous amount of money and expended a great many hours over the past ten months and we still have no answers. I don't think I'd mind so much if things had stabilized or showed even a little improvement, but each day seems a little worse."

"Have you talked to Baxter about it?" I asked.

He looked at me as if I had two heads. "Do ducks swim?"

"What does he say?"

Heavy sigh. "He keeps saying the same thing. 'Mr. Ball, there's little likelihood of this being a terminal illness. It's too narrow. Just get on with your life.'" He did a perfect imitation of Baxter. "What am I supposed to do? This hand is almost useless." He held the left hand out in front of him. "And the whole left arm is getting weaker. I'm having more and more trouble signing my name. By the way, you'll probably have to sign the charge slips when we go to Washington the end of the month. I'm writing—if you can call it that—with my right hand, and my signature doesn't resemble the one on the card. It's a good thing we got an extra card in your name last summer."

I concentrated on driving, but my mind focused on Bob's situation. Up to this point, his life reflected the choices he'd made. This was not a choice. Whatever he had was seriously invading day-to-day routines. I suddenly felt overwhelmed.

At the end of January, we attended the National Religious Broadcaster's Convention. For almost thirty years Bob had been part of this organization. Friendships ran deep. After attending the annual gathering, he always returned to work with renewed zeal for broadcasting, new ideas, and a fresh passion for the year ahead.

About two weeks before we left, he said, "You know, I'm a little leery about climbing into a tub-shower. Would you call the hotel and find out if they have any rooms with walk-in showers?"

He no longer had the strength in his left arm to catch himself if he started to slip or fall.

I booked a room in the old section of the hotel that offered walk-in showers and bought a wrist brace for him. Besides protecting his hand, it provided an unspoken reason for not writing.

"Hey, Bob! Good to see you. What's wrong with your hand?"

"Oh, Bobbie was practicing karate and I got in the way." Laughter.

"That old carpal tunnel thing, eh?"

"Could be. Doctor's checking it out."

There were few changes from previous years. We used room service more. Eating breakfast in our room meant we could prepare for the day at a slower pace. I kept Bob in sight in case he dropped something or needed an extra hand. He seemed to tire easily and occasionally opted out of a meeting.

"Well, the results of the MRI you had in January were consistent with the one done in May. Normal. No measurable change." Dr. Baxter lifted his eyes from the folder and looked at Bob. "How have you been feeling? Any new symptoms?"

"My writing, well, it was never good, now it's barely legible. Shirt buttons are impossible. Bobbie has to do them. I have a hard time with my tie. By the end of the day my left hand is swollen."

Baxter put him through the usual routines, checking grip strength and muscle strength in his arm. He made little comment as he examined Bob and scheduled him for a thermogram.

"Another test?"

"This is heat sensitive to detect irritation of the nerve roots."

I'm beginning to get irritated, Bob thought. *This seems to go on and on.*

In his summary Baxter noted: "left arm weakening—perhaps it would be prudent to send him to USC for an ALS trial." Once again he never mentioned this option to Bob or indicated he was now considering ALS.

We were walking. I knew there was something on Bob's mind, something he wanted to talk about. I waited.

"I think I've waited too long," His tone was low and unemotional.

I looked at him quizzically. "For what?"

"I can't sign my name anymore." His signature was free-flowing and very distinctive. A lefty, Bob was taught to write as if he were right-handed: slant the paper to the left. As a result, he wrote with his left wrist hooked above the paper, dragging his arm across what he had just written. A real mess before ballpoint pens. Sometimes he couldn't read his own notes—they were so badly smeared.

One summer during his teens, he went to a local secretarial school and learned to type. It changed his life. For the first time, he could turn in reports or term papers without ink smears. In college a lined yellow legal pad and printing made class notes legible. Now he depended on keyboarding for memos and to-do lists. No wonder he loved the computer.

"I should have gotten a signature stamp months ago while my

writing was still legible. Now I'm stuck. Any suggestions?"

"I'll get you one through the office supply company I use."

"How can you do that? They'll want an original copy of my signature on a blank sheet of white paper."

"I'll figure out a way. How about a second one with Bob?"

"That would be great if you could do it."

The signature was easy. I lifted it off an old check. "Bob" was harder. I hunted through old greeting cards, grateful I had kept them. Most of them were signed "Me," or "Your Sweetie," or "I Love You." Finally I found a Valentine signed simply: "Bob." I lifted it. In less than ten days Bob had his signature stamps. Hmmm, it's a good thing I never had criminal tendencies.

He was elated. "I'm not even going to ask how you did this. It's a wonderful gift, especially the 'Bob.' I don't know what I'd ever do without you, and I hope I never have to find out."

He was as happy over the two signature stamps as he would have been a year ago over a new camera. Funny how our level of expectation changes with the circumstances.

CHAPTER 8

*I*t was March. One full year since that first ominous twitch.

Bob sat in Baxter's office. After putting him through the various neurological maneuvers and checking grip strength, Baxter said, "I've reviewed the thermogram you had done last month of the upper torso (neck, shoulders and both arms). It definitely shows a difference between the two arms."

Well, duh, we already knew that!

"What do we do now?"

"Are you continuing to do exercises?"

"I keep a hand grip at my desk, nerf ball and silly putty at home, and last week we bought a rowing machine."

"Good. Good. Keep that up."

That was it.

Although he did not share his suspicions with Bob, he expressed them in his memo regarding that office visit: "possible motor neuron disease—check with USC re: neuro testing."

Once again he said nothing to Bob and told him to come back in two months.

I was buttoning Bob's shirt when he suddenly remarked, "I could live with this."

"With what?"

"Only having one arm that works."

His left arm hung limply at his side. Remnants of large-muscle strength remained but the small muscles of the fingers had lost all strength and movement.

"I've been watching Bob Dole. He has the use of only one arm. He carries that pen in his hand all the time. He seems to get along okay."

Hope. He still had hope. Although the shadow of ALS hung over everything, he hadn't given up. "Considering he's a senator and married to a knock-out wife, I'd say he's doing okay. We better hurry. We're not going to make it," I added.

We were meeting Dave and Penny for dinner. At a restaurant. An hour away. We were still adjusting to the driving thing. People in Southern California didn't seem to mind spending hours on the freeways. Two- to three-hour commute to work? A way of life. Drive an hour to church? No big deal. Travel an hour-and-a-half for dinner? Everybody does it.

At the restaurant, known for its steak and seafood, Bob ordered crepes with seafood in a strange sauce. He ate about half of it.

"Didn't like that too much, eh?" Dave joked.

"It was okay. As son David used to say, let's not have this again."

As we inched out of the parking lot, I asked, "Why ever did you order those crepes?"

It was a minute before he answered. "I don't have enough strength to use a knife anymore, and that was about the only thing on the menu I thought I could manage with a fork."

A chill ran through me. By now I was used to preparing meals he could manage with only a little help. At a restaurant in front of friends he wasn't about to ask for help.

So far he had been able to keep his physical limitations between us. Incredible as it sounds, no one at work knew or even suspected there was a problem. He wore a cock-up wrist brace to keep his left hand in a normal position. He made no attempt to hide the signature stamps, and no one questioned his constant use of them.

"Honey, how much longer do we have to wait before getting an answer? Not knowing what you're dealing with?" I turned to look at him. An elephant sat between us in the car.

By the first of May when Bob had his next appointment, his left arm was considerably weaker. The muscle wasting extended well into his arm and was clearly visible. In addition he was experiencing some neck pain and weakness in the right shoulder. Whatever was wrong, it seemed to be creeping up his left arm, across his shoulders, and working its way down his right arm.

"I think we should schedule a myelogram."

"A what?"

"A myelogram," Baxter replied. "Some spinal fluid is removed, contrast medium injected, and then radiology takes some pictures. It needs to be done in the hospital—an out-patient procedure. You'll have to check in and be assigned a bed, but the actual procedure only takes about an hour."

"Why are you suggesting this? Aren't the MRIs sufficient?"

"This will show if there's any obstruction in the spinal cord that may be blocking the normal flow of spinal fluid or any nerve root damage."

Bob shrugged, "If you think this is necessary."

"I'll have Jennifer schedule you. Stop at the desk on your way out."

When the memos from Baxter's office finally fell into our hands, what bothered us most was that the option of in-depth screening at an ALS center had never been suggested to Bob. We were never even told such a place existed. Why? I can't say. Was it because from the start Baxter had scoffed at Bob for assuming he might have ALS? Was it a reluctance to tell him potentially bad news? Like the ostrich with its head in the sand, did he think Bob would be better off if he didn't know he had an incurable disease? Sometimes people think you won't be able to cope with the facts so they keep them from you.

◆ ◆ ◆

I was sixteen when I found out I was illegitimate.

Born out of wedlock.

Of questionable heritage.

Oh, I always knew I was adopted. From the time I was old enough to talk, the term "adopted" had been part of my vocabulary.

I remember one rainy afternoon playing house with my sister. I was three or four. We had draped a sheet over the table in the dining room to make a little house. Time after time I had gone up and down the stairs at the direction of my older sibling to retrieve things from the bedroom for our "house." At four years my senior, my sister tended to assume a role of leadership bordering on bossy. She was the director. I was supposed to be the follower. After about ten trips climbing the stairs to fetch this or that for our table house, my short pudgy legs were beginning to complain.

"Go get the little chair in our bedroom."

"I'm tired," I whined.

"If we are going to have a proper house we need a chair. Go get it."

Wearily I climbed the stairs yet again. Struggling with the small wooden chair, I began to descend the stairs. As I neared the bottom, my sister yelled, "Hurry up!"

That was it. All appearance of sisterly compliance fled. Abruptly I sat down on the step balancing the chair in front of me. Glaring at my sister I snapped, "I mays be adopted, but I'm no Cinnerella!"

I continued to stare at the document in front of me. Reading it over and over again. The words burned into my mind: " whereabouts unknown."

My adopted mother, the one I called Mom, the one I loved, the one who was my mother, had never gone to college. She had no training in psychology or emotional well-being, but she always made me feel as if I were *special*.

They had to keep my sister; I was the *chosen* one.

They got stuck with my sister; I was *picked out*.

When Mom said they "picked me out," in my child's mind I conjured up something like the Ward's Catalog filled with pages and pages of pictures of sweet little babies. I imagined her turning the pages and asking Daddy, "What about this one? The one with brown hair and brown eyes."

When I asked her about it, she was always rather vague.

"All the people in charge of adopting babies knew just what we were looking for, and one day we got a phone call. They had the perfect baby for us. We were so excited. We went right away, and there you were. Our very own. Forever and ever."

As she said it, she'd throw her arms around me and hug me tight. I basked in the security of that hug.

When I got older, around five or six, I realized there had to be another mother somewhere, the one who 'borned' me and I began to ask more probing questions.

"Who was my other mother?"

"Did she want to keep me?"

"Why did she give me away?"

When I asked, Mom would always reply, "Sweetheart, when you were born your mother got very sick. Your father was very young and knew he couldn't take good care of you by himself, so he looked around for someone who could. And there we were, wanting another baby so very much, and here you are—ours forever."

Made perfect sense to me. Daddies didn't know how to take care of babies. Mommies did. In those days (before World War II) I didn't know anyone who had a mother working outside the home. Mothers stayed home to take care of the children. Fathers were shadowy figures who went to work early in the morning while you were still asleep and came home in the evening after you had gone to bed. Sometimes you only got to see them on Saturdays and Sundays.

My own daddy left the house at six-thirty every weekday morning and didn't get home until after six-thirty at night. Every so often we would eat dinner together at seven o'clock, but many days we ate before he got home. Surely a daddy couldn't be expected to care for a baby—and a girl at that! From time-to-time I would ask about that other daddy.

"Do you think he misses me?"

"Who, dear?"

"That other daddy?"

"What are you talking about?"

"You know, the one who was there when I was 'borned'?"

"Oh. I'm sure he does."

"Shouldn't we tell him I'm okay?"

"Uh, my goodness! Look what time it is! Time for you to do your practicing."

It was never said in so many words that my birth mother died, but it was implied and I never asked.

That morning as Daddy left for work he handed me an envelope. "Your adoption papers are in here. After school, I want you to stop by the Social Security office on Main Street. Show them the papers and give them this sealed copy of Mom's death certificate. There's supposed to be some money for you. Make sure you bring the adoption papers back home."

My adoption papers? I didn't know they existed. Typical sixteen-year-old, as soon as Daddy walked out the door, I sat on the edge of the bed and read the legal-looking document. As I read it one thing became very clear: Daddy never knew the story Mom had always told me. Now I read the words again. And again. And again. The names and places seared into my memory. They would never go away. They were there forever.

In that moment I devoured the words. My birth mother was sent out of state to a home for unwed mothers. That was often the course of action before abortion became legal and routine. The choices for my birth mother? Not many. She was probably told to "put that baby up for adoption and get on with your life." As for my father, following my birth father's name were the words "whereabouts unknown." So much for the grieving father I'd always conjured up. Obviously I was the result of, at most, a brief affair.

Was I upset by these findings? Strangely, no. Although the details of the appealing adoption story had been rewritten, the facts were only partially changed. I was brought into the world by default, by someone who cared enough to give me away. I was adopted by two people who loved me unconditionally, cared for me, nurtured me, taught me right from wrong, and respect for others. In this loving home the Bible was the foundation for faith and practice. I learned about the God of the Bible, who loved me and gave His Son for me. Even as a child I recognized my own sinfulness and grew to understand that only by God's redeeming grace could I be part of His family. A child of God by adoption—a term I thoroughly understood.

Loving God, loving parents, loving home. What more could a child want?

◆ ◆ ◆

A week later we checked into the hospital. Bob signed the pre-requisite consent forms and we were escorted to a room. He donned the appropriate designer gown and then he was gone. I waited. In a little less then an hour he was wheeled back in.

"Now remember," said the hefty nurse as she transferred him to the hospital bed, "keep your head elevated. Do not lie flat. I'll be back in about thirty minutes to check on you."

"How'd it go?" I asked once we were alone.

"I suppose fine. When you don't know what to expect it's hard to judge."

"Are you feeling okay?"

He nodded. The room was warm. He dozed. The nurse came in, checked his vitals, and was gone. We waited.

In about an hour Dr. Baxter came in. He sat on the foot of the bed. After inquiring about Bob's present condition, he said, "So far the results appear unremarkable. There's no evidence of any ob-struction or any damage to the spinal nerves."

There was silence finally broken by Bob. "What now?"

Baxter folded his arms across his belly. "We could try steroids."

I couldn't believe what I was hearing. It had now been fifteen months since Bob felt the first symptoms. Fifteen months of fas-ciculations and muscle wasting. Fifteen months of watching Bob lose the battle to this unknown assailant. How in the world could Baxter suggest a treatment when we didn't have a diagnosis.

"What do you think, Honey?" Bob looked at me from the bed.

I lost it.

In retrospect I probably should have chosen my words with great-er care, but I blurted out, "I think it's time we stopped fooling around and found out what's causing the muscle wasting and weakness."

Oops.

Baxter was off the bed in a flash. "Fooling around! Is that what you think I've been doing? Fooling around? After all my efforts you're an ungrateful %@#! What the %&@ do you know? What degrees do you hold in medicine? What good is it going to do if you put a %@# label on him? Do you think that will cure him?" By this time he was pacing the room, glaring at me and waving his arms. Practically snorting.

Bob rose up on one elbow. There, in his hospital gown, my beloved Prince Valiant came to my defense.

"Nobody speaks to my wife that way. You owe her an apology."

There was a moment of awkward silence while Baxter continued to glare at me. "I'm sorry. I shouldn't have raised my voice." The words were icy.

"I'm sorry." My voice was level, but I was determined. "I shouldn't have used that terminology. I know you've conducted months of tests in an effort to locate the cause of the problem, and we are grateful for all the work you've done. We know what it's not. Now it's time to find out what we're dealing with, what's causing this."

Visibly irritated, the doctor turned towards Bob and remarked, "We'll talk about it at your next office visit." He hurried out of the room.

I grimaced and looked at Bob. "I'm sorry, Honey. I probably shouldn't have said that. I hope I didn't speak out of turn."

"You're pretty gutsy. It needed to be said." He grinned and then added, "Perhaps not in those exact words." He paused, "I think we've seen the last of Baxter."

That afternoon Bob called Sam Costene.

CHAPTER 9

*D*etroit. The room was the same as thousands of other hotel rooms: small, without a view or anything else to make it memorable. Just a place to sleep—but it would remain forever in our memory banks.

It was mid-June. In thirty minutes Bob was scheduled for a screening at the Neuromuscular Clinic in Henry Ford Hospital. Wait a minute. Aren't there ALS clinics in California? Of course. Respected ones. Then why were we in Michigan? You can't just walk into a clinic and say, "Hey, I think I have ALS." You need a referral with a preliminary workup. Since Dr. Baxter apparently thought about making such a referral, but, for whatever reason, appeared reluctant to actually do it, Bob had turned to Sam Costene for help. A month earlier we had our explosive confrontation with Baxter and now, thanks to Sam's kindness and intervention, here we were in the Motor City.

I buttoned Bob's shirt and helped him smooth the tail of it neatly into his slacks.

"Nervous?" I asked.

"A little. Mostly I'm looking forward to some answers." He kissed me on the cheek as I buttoned his waistband and zipped his fly, a maneuver he could no longer manage.

We walked the short distance to the hospital. The clinic was crowded with people in progressive stages of the disease. With walkers, wheelchairs, and respirators, they were a cross section of the population—old, young, male, female—all in one place.

I went into neutral. The next two days were a blur. I would remember little, just bits and pieces.

Once again, Bob was poked and prodded, questioned and studied. He was subjected to EMG and nerve conduction studies. Late in the afternoon of that first day we sat in the reception area waiting to be summoned for yet another EMG. A young man stuck his head in and called, "Mr. Ball?"

We both got up to follow him, and he said to me, "You'll have to wait out here."

"Does he have to disrobe?"

"Oh, yes." He held up one hand. "But I promise we'll take good care of him."

"He needs help getting out of his clothes."

"Oh, ah, well," he stammered, "I guess you better come."

I remember thinking, *Don't other patients need help when they come for an initial evaluation? Is it unusual to be this far along without a diagnosis?*

Friday afternoon, day two, we met for consultation. After sixteen months, we heard what we already suspected: Bob had Lou Gehrig's disease. Only now it was official. He had a label. No longer was there a glimmer of hope that it might be something else.

"How much time do I have left?" That was Bob: Let's get right to the heart of it.

The doctor was equally forthright in responding. "Considering the progression of the disease to this point, probably eighteen months without intervention."

"Intervention?"

"A feeding tube can add months to your life when it becomes difficult to chew and swallow. It also will protect you from aspirating food or drink into your lungs, which can result in serious complications, like pneumonia. You don't want that. You don't want to get any kind of respiratory infection."

By this time the social worker had joined us. "You can go on a ventilator. A respirator," she added, "can extend your life much longer."

"But what kind of life would it be?" Bob interjected. "Trapped in a body that doesn't move; not being able to speak. Feeding tube, probably. I don't want to starve to death or put the family through that. Ventilator, no. I do not want to go on a ventilator. I'm not afraid of death—that was settled long ago—but I don't look forward to the process of dying. I don't like to think about gasping for breath. About not being able to breathe. About smothering."

"Oh, no," they answered in unison. The doctor continued, "No gasping for breath or feeling of suffocation. If you need it, there is medication to keep you comfortable. Mr. Ball, you and your wife and family need time to discuss this. If you decide not to go on a ventilator, you need to make that decision known to your doctor and never ever call 911. Regardless of your wishes, paramedics will make every effort to save your life and put you on a ventilator even if you wave an official document under their noses.

"ALS is a progressive disease. You are going to get worse. You will become totally dependent on others. Except for bladder control and eye-movement, you will lose all muscle control and movement."

An uncomfortable stillness settled over the room. No one spoke. No one stirred. I couldn't look at Bob.

The doctor turned to me and continued, "We'll refer Mr. Ball to the ALS Research Center closest to you. They will monitor his condition and assign someone to advise you. As his condition worsens he will be more dependent on you. You are going to need help. Don't hesitate to ask for assistance."

I nodded. I couldn't speak. The elephant was lodged in my throat.

The doctor's voice softened, "It's been obvious to our staff that the bond between you is extraordinary and your faith is strong. Thanks for giving us the opportunity to get to know you. Now, do you have any questions?"

I looked at Bob. He shook his head. I turned to the doctor, "How do you do this day after day? ALS is such a hopeless diagnosis. There certainly can't be much satisfaction for you at the end of the day."

"It does get depressing. I could be flip and say somebody has to do it, but with all the data we accumulate and trials we conduct, the hope that keeps us going is that we will find a cure. Maybe even in your lifetime." He smiled at Bob. "Now, you've got good months left. Take advantage of them. Do something you enjoy."

As we walked back to the hotel I clutched Bob's arm. A profound silence hung between us. Finally he spoke, "Now listen, no tears. We've still got a lot of living to do. I don't want you or anybody else to feel sorry for me, to pity me. We know what we're dealing with; *now* let's get on with life. After all, there is a bright side."

I looked at him dubiously. "Well, I sure missed it."

"You don't have to worry about me getting Alzheimer's," he replied with a grin.

The next day we visited Greenfield Village, home of the Henry Ford Museum. I know we went. I have the ticket stubs to prove it. But I have no memory of being there. None. Late that afternoon we flew back to Los Angeles, and, since the doctor encouraged him to do something with the good months left, we started looking for a motorhome.

◆　◆　◆

"What does it look like?"

"Here." He shoved a piece of paper under my nose. "You see, one side of the tent fits over the station wagon so you can use the bed of the wagon for more room. We could put the girls up in there to sleep and we'd sleep in the tent."

"What about the baby?"

"He could stay in the tent with us."

I looked skeptical.

"If we zip the sleeping bags together there'd be plenty of room for you and me *and* the baby. Besides it's an inexpensive vacation and we get to see some beautiful country."

Two kids from the city. What did we know about camping? We bought the tent, sleeping bags, a Coleman stove and lantern, and left for a weekend of adventure in the wilderness, well, county park. David was six weeks old.

Rule #1: Make a list of must-haves. Check it off.

Margie looked worried. Almost four, she took her role as big sister very seriously. Both little sister and brother were crying. Bob walked back and forth with Carolyn against his shoulder. We had forgotten her pacifier *and* her "bankie." She was desolate. She would doze off on Bob's shoulder, only to waken with a start when he tried to put her down. David, wailing from who knows what, hung on my shoulder while I patted his back. We must have looked like a scene out of *The Grapes of Wrath.* Fellow campers cast furtive glances at us, silently hoping this racket wouldn't continue into the night.

After much walking, jiggling, and soothing humming, the two youngest fell into a restless sleep. With Margie in her pjs, I read her a story by the light of the lantern on the picnic table. I had to admit the scene was rather pleasant.

She whispered in my ear, "I have to go potty."

At home you take this announcement casually. Here, in the dark, it was a major move. I picked her up in one arm (she was barefoot) and, with my free hand, grabbed the small flashlight we had snatched out of the car. It glowed dimly. We set off for the pit toilet.

The black hole looked even bigger and blacker with this wispy child perched on the edge. I clamped one arm protectively around her shoulder and held the flashlight in the other hand.

"I'm done," she announced.

Now what? How was I going to get toilet paper with no hands? I carefully put the flashlight on the bench and reached for the paper. The flashlight began to roll towards the black hole. I lunged for it. Margie rocked backwards. I grabbed her with my other hand. Splat! The impact must have jarred the weak batteries into life for now the black hole emitted an eerie light.

"Mama, I'm done!"

Her little derriere glowed in the darkness. I started to giggle.

As I picked her up she said, "You forgot the flashlight."

Stifling the rising laughter, I replied, "I think we'll just leave it here for the rest of the campers."

Bob was reading in the pool of light from the lantern.

"If," I began, "we *ever* go camping again, we will need a large, square flashlight with a handle."

"Where's the one from the car?"

"Providing illumination for all who seek relief during the night."

He began to laugh.

Rule #2: When camping, never pitch your tent on an incline.

The muffled sounds of a baby's cry roused me from fitful sleep. David. The ground under me was hard, and there seemed to be a rock beneath my shoulder. I reached out for the baby. He wasn't there. I felt around. No baby. I could hear him crying, more insistent now.

I sat up. "Bob! Wake up!" I whispered, not wanting to wake the girls. "Bob!" I shook him.

"Umm."

You could take the mattress out from under him or set fire to it. The sound of blasting sirens could wake the neighborhood; he'd sleep through it all.

"Bob!" I hissed in a stage whisper.

"What?" he answered sleepily.

"The baby's gone. I can hear him, but it's so dark in here I can't find him."

At this he sat up. "I don't hear him."

"Well, he's stopped now." By this time our eyes were growing accustomed to the dimness. "Help me find him."

"I think he's at the bottom of the sleeping bag." He pointed to a small lump. Crawling headfirst into the bag, he retrieved the lump, and emerged with a sleepy baby.

"Is he all right?"

"Seems to be fine; must have slid down. Hmmm. I guess I did set this up on a slope."

Rule #3: Never store a wet tent.

The next morning the rains set in. Reluctantly Bob agreed we should probably go home. With the children snug in the car, we quickly broke camp and hit the road. Any unpleasant memories evaporated rapidly, and in about six weeks we were ready to try again.

"What's that smell?" I asked as we traveled towards the campground, one with flush toilets.

"I don't know. I've got the vent open; must be something outside."

As we laid out the tent at the campground, we realized the smell was us. The tent was covered with mildew, in fact, some parts were still damp.

"Oh yuck!" I exclaimed. "Are we going to be able to sleep in this?"

"Hey, it's sunny and warm. It will probably dry out by tonight."

He started pounding in the tent pegs. Suddenly a geyser shot into the air.

"Whoa! What in the world!" Bob yanked the tent out of the way and ran to get the park attendant. By the time they got back, the geyser had subsided and water was bubbling out of the ground forming a lake. Part of the tent was soaked. The park employee found the valve and turned off the water supply.

"Don't worry about it," he said. "This happens at least once a week. Whoever designed this place set the pipes too close to the surface. I'll help you move."

With such a dubious start to life in the great outdoors, nobody would have raised an eyebrow if we planned all subsequent vacations at the Hilton. We persevered; rather, Bob did. We moved into a small trailer, a bigger trailer, and, by the time David was six, into a twenty-six-foot Airstream. Lasting memories. Good memories.

◆　◆　◆

Bob would have liked a Blue Bird or even a large Winnebago, but reality set in. I would eventually do most of the driving. It had to be something small enough for me to handle comfortably. We had always admired the well-built Chinook. It was fully self-contained and, at twenty-one feet, a size I could manage. We began to check the classifieds.

Before Bob laid out money for a "luxury" item (something we didn't need), he had to justify the purchase in his own mind. I would have gladly used all of our savings or taken a second mortgage on the house to buy him anything he wanted, but we had to talk about it.

"If we had an RV, you could fix meals and we wouldn't need to go to a restaurant."

"That's true."

"It has its own bathroom, so you could help me."

I nodded. We had purchased a zipper pull, but it didn't tuck in his shirt or fasten the button at his waist. An increasingly difficult task with only one hand.

"I'd rather be in my own bed, and I wouldn't have to lug luggage around."

"Bob. Get it. If we buy one that's used, we can always get our money out of it."

A note lay on Bob's desk when he got back from lunch: "Call about the chinwok."

Bob questioned the young girl who took the message. "What is this about?"

"Some man called while you were out. He wants you to call him back. He said it was about the chinwok."

"That's what he said? 'Chinwok'?"

"Oh yes. He even spelled it for me: c-h-i-n-w-o-k," she spelled.

Bob turned on his heels before he permitted the grin to creep across his face. He called about the Chinook: "C-H-I-N-double O-K." A used motorhome on a Ford chassis, with 9,000 miles on it. It was immaculate. We bought it and promptly dubbed it "Chinwok."

The first night we used it was a nightmare. Bob couldn't turn over in his sleeping bag. We are so accustomed to movement we don't realize how much the muscles of the body depend on each other. A simple task like turning over requires the muscles of the upper torso to work in unison with the legs. In a king-sized bed there was no problem—his upper body just followed his legs. The confines of a sleeping bag made that simple maneuver impossible. We got little sleep. Scrap the sleeping bag.

The next day we stopped at Penney's and bought sheets and a decent pillow (I forgot his). As we were checking out, the cashier noticed the brace on Bob's wrist. Conversationally she asked, "Carpal tunnel?"

I barely looked up but muttered, "I wish."

As we walked back to the motorhome, Bob spoke. His voice was firm. "Don't do that."

"What?"

"What you said to the clerk back there."

"But I *do* wish it was carpal tunnel."

By this time we were back in Chinwok. He dropped the bag on the couch and put his hand on my shoulder. "So do I. But it's not, and it's not going to change."

Unbidden, the tears began to run down my face. It was the first time since our visit to Henry Ford that I had given way to tears in Bob's presence. He pulled me close, and when he spoke his voice was full of love and tenderness. "Ah, Bobbie Jean, remember, I said no tears. You've got to be tough. If you fall apart on me I don't think I can make it. Like it says in Proverbs: 'The heart of her husband does safely trust in her.' I'm trusting you with my life. Okay?"

I nodded. "But…"

He put his finger on my lips. "Shhh. We're not going to dwell on tomorrow. We're going to enjoy today, every minute of it. After all," he shrugged, "I've got you, this RV, and a cast-iron skillet under the seat. What more could I ask for? Let's hit the road!"

I couldn't help but smile. With that he started up Chinwok and we pulled out of the parking lot. The sun was shining, the scenery breathtaking, my love was at my side, and for the moment the elephant had submerged into the teapot. I knew it was lurking, but maybe it would drown in the tea. I looked out the window so Bob wouldn't notice the tears that kept blurring my vision.

CHAPTER 10

*O*ver the years Bob had been a sounding board, the ear that listened to complaints, a neutral counsel for burdened souls. People just seemed to gravitate to him with their frustrations or sorrows. Once, when we were walking, he said, "Everybody dumps on me, but I don't, or can't, feel comfortable sharing with anyone except you." Now he had to divulge the diagnosis of ALS not only to family, but to his close-knit office staff as well as colleagues and friends. And he had to do it himself. And soon.

It had been rather easy to keep Bob's gradual decline from the children; they were all out of state. However, after all these months, they knew something was wrong. Our evasive answers when they asked about the wrist brace he wore constantly and the frequent doctor visits had put them on edge. Now we faced the grim task of telling them, letting them know before we told anyone else. They were dismayed to hear the diagnosis. Like many in this post-Lou Gehrig generation, they knew it was *bad*, but then, how could someone who looked so healthy, who was so healthy, have something incurable? It took a while for the reality of what we were all facing to settle in.

With the family brought up to speed on his condition, he turned to the unpleasant job of notifying coworkers, business colleagues, and others he had bonded with over the years. He dreaded the task. He set about composing a letter to send to those outside the office.

"My biggest concern is that people will feel sorry for me," he opined, looking up from his keyboard. "I really don't want to be pitied."

When he broke the news to the staff, there was instant shock and disbelief followed by a heartfelt show of support. Even a promise of: "You've got a job here until your body reaches room temperature!" A generous sentiment uttered in the throes of compassion. I took it simply as an expression of encouragement; Bob, a man of his word, took it at face value.

It was July. We planned a trip to Oregon and Washington, not just to visit with the children, but to assure them our faith was not shaken. More than ever we trusted in the sovereignty of God. We packed up Chinwok and headed north. We camped our way through Northern California and into Central Oregon. High desert country. Made to order vistas for the Chamber of Commerce. An idyllic spot Bob had chosen for retirement. It was a bittersweet time—sweet with the memory of tranquil interludes, bitter with the realization that the anticipated retirement would never happen.

Chinwok behaved flawlessly. The benefit of a fully self-contained vehicle is, well, it's fully self-contained. Enough water, battery power, and holding tank to keep you going without hooking up to outside utilities for several days. After two nights of roughing it, when we stopped at an RV park in Bend, Bob stepped out to connect Chinwok to the electricity, water, and sewer available at each site. At the sound of his voice, I turned towards the open window.

"Hon, can you come out here for a minute?" he spoke softly. Thinking he had seen a deer or an eagle, I quietly opened the door and stepped outside.

"I can't stoop down to make the connections."

I looked at him blankly.

"I can't balance. I'm afraid I'll end up on my tush, and I won't be able to get up."

It had happened once before.

We had a bionic chair at home. Shaped like a checkmark with padding but no legs, it sat directly on the floor. It hugged the contours of the body and was amazingly relaxing. After a full day at the office, Bob would plop into it, watch the evening news, and then rock backwards until his upper torso was parallel with the floor and his knees hung over the lower edge of the chair.

Last week he managed to get into it. When he tried to get out he could not.

"Bobbie, I think I'm stuck."

His left arm was useless, and the upper muscles of his right arm like rubber—without enough strength to help him get up and out of the chair.

At Henry Ford I had been cautioned never to help him up by the arms. The muscles were so weakened his arm could easily pull out of the shoulder socket. I reached around his chest and tried to help. Not a chance; especially from that angle.

I tried again. This time we counted. "Okay, at the count of three, try and push off with your legs while I lift your body up."

Who did I think I was kidding? Just imagine standing two feet away from a barrel on the floor weighing almost two hundred pounds and trying to get your arms around it to lift it.

"One, two, *three!*" His back lifted about two inches from the chair and fell back. I crashed down on top of him.

I pulled myself out of the tangled mass and sat on the floor. For a minute we just looked at each other. Then, with a half-hearted laugh, I asked, "What are we going to do? Do I need to call somebody for help?"

"Let's see if I can scoot this closer to the couch. Maybe I can get out that way. You push."

We tried. The chair began to turn in circles. He ended up back where he started. I was absolutely no help. For the first time in my life I wished for the bulk of a Wagnerian opera singer.

"That's not gonna' work. I'm just going to have to fall out."

Without waiting for comment, he tumbled out the side of the chair unto his knees. Now what? He was in a crawling position, but his arms were unable to offer any help. Crawling was out of the question. Carefully, I crept underneath him and positioned myself under his chest.

"That's good! That's good! I think we can do it."

The six feet to the couch seemed to stretch the length of a football field. We inched toward it. In this bizarre manner we crept across the room. We must have looked like some alien space creature with eight legs, but only six worked. Finally reaching the couch, he rested his chin on it.

"Here, put my arms up on the couch."

I crawled out from under him and carefully put his arms on the couch. The left immediately slithered off. I put it up again and this time held it gently in place. With both arms on the couch, he literally swam his upper body unto the couch, managed to swivel his body around, and sat down. I plopped down next to him. We were both exhausted. What do you do? Cry? Laugh? We sat on the couch hugging and laughing at the weird spectacle we must have made.

The bionic chair was left to gather dust.

We didn't want a repeat, especially out in the open among strangers. I followed Bob around to the side of the RV. This was his job. Something he had always done. While I mucked about inside getting dinner ready, he'd work outside connecting power cords and hoses. I knew he felt humiliated to have to come get me.

I plugged in the electrical cord, attached the water line, and was trying to figure out the sewage connection as Bob hovered nearby giving instructions.

At that moment a middle-aged couple strolled past and the man, seeing Bob supervising while I did the work, remarked, "Teaching the little lady to take care of the nitty gritty, eh? Good idea!" They laughed as they walked on by. Once again I saw the look of resignation pass over Bob's face.

An elephant peered from the window of the RV.

We pulled Chinwok into Marge and Steve's driveway. Two little bodies hurtled out the screen door. Amazing how deeply you love those grandchildren. Their eyes shining with delight, they could hardly wait to drag Grandpa into the house. After hugs and kisses and small chitchat, Marge said, "We've remodeled the downstairs bath."

"Come on, Grandpa, I'll show you." Stephen grabbed Bob's hand and led him down to the basement.

At the bottom of the stairs Bob turned. "Carolyn!"

The boys jumped up and down with glee. We had pulled it off. Known to me, but a surprise to Bob, Carrie had flown into Portland to surprise her daddy and spend time with her siblings. Just as they reached that comfortable phase in life where parents become friends and confidants, when Dad's advice is actually sought, they would have to say goodbye. The three of them, now adults with responsibilities of their own, would have to prepare for the loss of their father. Too soon. Too soon.

On their own they grappled with the situation—a dad who would get worse and a mom who would need help taking care of him. Bottom line, Carolyn was the only one unencumbered by family. Like it or not, she was elected. She would fly back to South Carolina, take care of business, pack things up, and drive to California. We balked at the idea of asking her to put her life on hold, but it was already decided. She would become cook, shopper, helper, and, when the situation called for it, comic relief. Our blessing.

CHAPTER 10

It was late in the day when we pulled into the RV campground on the Oregon coast. Bob stayed in Chinwok, while I hooked up the utilities. Actually he was hiding. If he didn't show his face there would be less chance of facing the same situation we encountered in Central Oregon.

"Hey, Hon, let's walk down to the bluff and watch the sunset," I called through the screen door. In a quieter voice I asked, "It's going to be cold when the sun goes down. Do you need some help with your jacket?"

We walked the short distance to the bluff. Already the lowering sun was shooting spectacular rays of light into the darkening blue sky. The scene before us was filled with achingly familiar memories. Children and dogs raced on the hard-packed sand left by the receding tide. Parents stood nearby occasionally shouting, "Watch where you're going!" or "Never turn your back on the ocean!" Closer to us, where the sand was dry and soft, couples watched the setting sun, sitting arm-in-arm on logs left by winter storms.

As the sun slipped below the far horizon, I said, "Want to walk on the beach?" Neither of us said it, but we were both thinking *one last time.*

"That would be nice."

I held his good arm as we walked down the few steps to the beach. We stepped off into the sand.

Mistake.

Bob's foot sank into the ever-shifting sand. I felt his body lurch.

"You okay?" I asked softly.

He did not reply. With a look of dogged determination, he managed about six paces.

"I can't do this. We need to go back."

Even though the sun had dropped below the horizon, the sky before us, to the West, was still awash with light. I kept a firm grip on Bob's arm as we turned to go back. The sky to the East was already dark. We headed toward the blackness. Gloom settled over us. With an effort, I shoved thoughts of the present and future away and pulled up the past. We were at the beach. A place filled with countless family memories. Time to lighten the moment.

"Remember when we first brought Cleo to the beach?"

Bob smiled, then shook his head. With a laugh he said, "I thought we lost her."

◆ ◆ ◆

"A boy should have a dog," Bob stated.

"He's going to be six in a couple of weeks," I said. "Think we should get him one for his birthday? Maybe a German shepherd?"

We started looking in the classifieds.

"Listen to this." I read the ad: "'Puppies. Black lab, German shepherd, more. Three to six months.'"

"That sounds promising. Why don't you give them a call?"

I did and we set a time to view the puppies.

Bob and I followed the owner into the house. In place of a dining table, there was a baby crib chock full of puppies—five, maybe six pups of different breeds. Although this was a curious situation, it never occurred to us to ask where they came from. The German shepherd was bigger than the others. The young man hoisted him out of the crib and sat him on the floor in front of us. "This is Brutus."

His feet were huge. He was going to be big. He sat on the floor and stared at us with a steady, cold gaze. Frankly, he scared the stuffing out of me. Guard dog? Super choice. Family pet? I didn't think so.

"Is that a beagle?" I pointed to a pup that looked like a beagle but was already as big as a fully grown beagle.

"No," he said as he put the German shepherd back and lifted that dog out. "This is a black and tan coonhound. She'll get about as big as a lab. Very friendly."

All the experts say do your research on the breed before you buy. Good advice. We didn't follow it. Cleo, short for Cleopatra—don't ask me why we hung that moniker on her—became part of the family.

We soon learned what a black and tan coonhound does—it hunts. She was a hound dog. When she got on the scent of a 'possum or raccoon, she would tear through the adjoining stretch of woods baying as she ran.

One afternoon we got a call from the neighbor. The Weckmans were a middle-aged couple with no children and no pets. Their yard was always immaculate.

"Barbara? Do you know your dog has been stealing our ducks?"

"She what?"

"I know this sounds kind of silly, but we have, had, a duck and three ducklings in the garden. One by one, the ducklings disappeared. I just caught your dog with the third one in her mouth. They're only plastic, but we rather liked them."

I was very gracious, I hope, expressing regret and offering to replace them, but I could hardly contain the laughter. A hunting dog? Maybe she was a bird dog, but plastic? Either she was desperate for quarry or not awfully bright. In time, we came to the conclusion it was the latter.

The first time we took Cleo to the beach turned into an adventure we'd never forget. We had parked our vacation trailer at the beach in a private campground that offered longterm parking. It made a terrific retreat. Now here we were with a new member of the family. Wherever we went, Cleo went.

We put her in the back of the station wagon and quickly learned she was a terrible traveler. She walked all the way to the beach—marching round and round in the rear of the wagon. During the two-hour trip we took turns shouting, "Cleo! Lie down!" which she did for about thirty seconds. She panted, drooled, slobbered on the children, and tried to crawl into the back seat. As soon as we unloaded the car, we grabbed Cleo's leash, clipped it on her collar, and hiked the short distance to the beach.

"Keep her on the leash until we get to the hard-packed sand," Bob admonished.

When we hit that smooth stretch of beach, David asked, "Do you think it's okay to take off her leash?"

Bob looked at the uncrowded expanse. "Oh, sure."

David unhooked her leash.

She took off like a gazelle. I had never seen her run that fast. She flew. In unison, we yelled, "Cleo!" We whistled. We clapped. We called her name until we were hoarse. At first David tried to catch up with her, but his six-year-old legs were no match for this demon rocket. We stood and watched in stunned silence as she hurtled down the open beach, became a little speck and then disappeared.

David, on the verge of tears, turned towards his dad just as Margie pointed down the beach and exclaimed, "Look! Here she comes!" Once again we watched the speck get larger and larger until, with tongue hanging out the side of her mouth, she reached us, passed us, and headed in the opposite direction.

This time our frantic calls brought Cleo back. As she galloped towards us, she suddenly braked. Standing stiff-legged, the hackles on her back rose as she began to bark. Only then did we notice the object of her barking: two nuns in black, flowing habits sitting on a log. Offering apologies to the frightened-looking pair, we snapped on her leash and headed for the RV park. Cleo spent the rest of the day beside the campfire, alternately snoozing and cleaning the sand from between her toes.

She loved the beach.

◆　◆　◆

Bob and I settled in for the night with precious memories of long-past family times filling our dreams. How blessed we'd been. How blessed we were.

The next morning, we cut inland and took the interstate towards California. That summer we crammed in as much travel with Chinwok as we possibly could: two extended vacations, a couple of one-night camping trips, and several day treks. We savored every minute.

In the end, our final trip to Oregon in early September was too much. The last four hundred miles of the return trip found me in the driver's seat. By the time we got home, Bob was exhausted. So tired, that when we parked in the driveway he let me help him into the house and into bed without a word. It had been a great summer, and we would treasure the memories. Chinwok had served us well.

The staff at the Ford clinic had told us to call if we needed anything or had any questions. Now I did. We needed a disability placard from the DMV, and the ALS Association offered a set of practical manuals to anyone diagnosed with the disease. Both agencies required some form of documentation stating a person did, indeed, have ALS. I placed a call to Theresa, the intake counselor assigned to Bob.

"Hi, Theresa. This is Robert Ball's wife. We were there in June. I need confirmation that Bob was seen at the clinic and diagnosed with ALS. Could you send that to me?"

"Of course. How's Mr. Ball doing?"

"Physically? A little worse each day."

She asked if I had a fax, and within two hours I was reading a confirming letter. The room slowly receded, and the only thing that existed was the letter I held in my hands.

> Mr. Robert Ball is diagnosed with having Amyotrophic Lateral Sclerosis (Lou Gehrig's Disease). This is a progressive motor neuron disease, which affects the voluntary muscles throughout the body. ALS is a catastrophic disease and is terminal.

The word terminal leapt off the page. It echoed and reechoed. Terminal, terminal, terminal, terminal. I knew the disease was fatal. I had read it. I heard it from the doctors. It was in my head. Suddenly, it was in my gut. Bob was terminal. I stared at the word. In a flash, the raw truth set in. He was going to die; I was going to lose him. I don't know how long I sat there, but the elephant of despair was crushing. The shock slowly passed and action set in. Methodically I copied the fax and filed it away.

We seldom kept secrets from each other.

This would be one of them.

I never showed the letter to Bob.

CHAPTER 11

$\mathscr{A}$s the news of Bob's illness became known publicly, phone calls, cards, and letters began to trickle in. The trickle soon became an overwhelming deluge. Letters from colleagues expressed appreciation for a life of integrity and faithfulness, coupled with sadness for the ordeal he now faced. The ones that brought him closest to tears came out of the blue. Not from business associates but from individuals he had mentored early in their careers or those who had turned to him when they needed a helping hand. Perhaps most poignant of all were accounts of lives changed as they sat under his Bible teaching years earlier in Sunday School.

There were a couple of bizarre ones. I guess that's expected when you cast a long shadow. One said, "Confess! You must have some awful sin in your life to bring about this punishment." Another read, "Well, the great Bob Ball is finally getting his!" I couldn't believe anyone would ever write and send such a message.

"Whatever did you do to him?" I asked.

"I have no idea. Some slight or other, I suppose. It really doesn't matter. Maybe it made him feel better to put it in writing."

In the usual way he dismissed irrelevant things, he crumpled up the piece of paper, threw it away, and promptly put it behind him.

Once, early in our marriage, we had attended a conference where the featured speaker, a godly man, spoke about the love of God. Afterwards I sat gathering my things and only halfway listening to the conversation going on around me. Bob greeted some friends and then turned to me and asked, "Ready to go?"

Before I could respond, a rather portly man stopped at the end of the row preventing any possibility of escape.

Bob glanced up. "Hi, Mark. I'd like you to meet my wife, Bobbie. Hon, this is Mark Dever."

I looked up with a smile of greeting on my face.

Without acknowledging my presence, he stared at Bob with steely eyes and in an equally steely voice said, "Every day I pray that God will strike you dead. That you will disappear off the face of the planet."

The smile froze on my face. Was he serious?

"Well, Mark, you do what you have to do," Bob replied easily.

Mark turned and, as he walked away, I recovered enough to say, "Nice meeting you!"

Bob looked at me with raised eyebrows and mouthed the words, 'nice meeting you?' A broad grin settled over his face.

I shrugged. "He caught me by surprise and my manners just kicked in; merely an automatic response. I've never heard anybody say anything like that! What in the world was that all about?"

"He's a rather bitter competitor. Don't worry about him. Come on. Let's go."

As always, Bob dealt with the situation and erased it. No wonder he slept like a baby!

By the end of summer, eighteen months after the first menacing twitch, we had a glimpse of the future. The insatiable Pac-Man crept methodically and leisurely up the left arm, chomping at the pathways that carried nutrients to the muscles and destroying them. Without a source of nourishment, the muscles slowly starved and died. Bob's arm swung limply from the shoulder. Useless. No matter how hard he willed it to move, nothing happened.

No longer satisfied with this leisurely pace, the disease now raced across his shoulders and, with alarming speed, started down his right arm. With each new day, some movement was affected. He battled fiercely, doggedly, not willing to give an inch to this indifferent foe. It was a losing battle.

I dreaded the inevitable; the day Bob couldn't drive anymore. Wheels were a symbol of manhood. The first tangible sign of independence. The story of our life together could be recalled by the car we owned at the time—twenty-two in all. Each car was considered a treasure and cared for as if it were the very first and would be the very last. They were washed and waxed, vacuumed and polished, serviced on schedule and fussed over. Service records were stored away, along with a legacy of pictures of the proud owner standing next to his vehicle *du jour.*

When we moved to California, where the water was hard and left splotches of mineral deposit if allowed to air dry, I stood at the ready when he washed the car.

"Okay. You got the towel?"

A stack of old, soft bath towels rested on the back seat—not on the driveway where they might pick up some grit.

"Got it," I said, holding a towel in my hands.

You had to work fast in this sunny clime, wetting, soaping, rinsing, drying. It became a ritual we both enjoyed. Working together under cloudless skies, Bob cleaning the upper parts I couldn't reach, while I worked on the lower part. It reminded me of dusting with Mom when I was a child.

"How come I always have to dust the chair rungs and the baseboards?"

"Because you're closer to them, dear."
"When I grow up I won't have to do the bottoms."
Here I was, all grown up and still doing the bottoms.

When Bob first lost the muscle strength in his left arm and hand, we hunted for a steering wheel spinner—a knob attached to the wheel that made turning with one hand a breeze. They were all the rage when we were in high school. Unable to find them anywhere, we were beginning to think they had gone the way of big fins and acres of chrome until Bob discovered one in an auto accessory catalog. When he tried to place an order, we found out why we never saw any—they were illegal in California.

My guess is that we probably could have gotten one with a medical disability claim. When I mentioned this to Bob, he responded, "What's the point? By the time we jump through all the hurdles I probably won't have enough muscle strength left to use it anyway."

We both knew he shouldn't be driving. But he still managed. With his left arm resting in his lap, his right hand clutched the bottom of the steering wheel. Since he was unable to lift his right arm anymore, when he approached a turn he would exert pressure on the steering wheel with his knees and move his right hand in increments to turn the wheel. Thanks to power steering and automatic transmission he was able to cope.

I prayed fervently when he left in the morning and held my breath if I heard the wail of sirens. Each day I waited for him to acknowledge it was too risky to drive anymore. It would mean giving up that initial symbol of manhood, the first vestige of independence.

Now that we weren't able to take long evening strolls, discussions, those emptying-of-the-soul talks, had moved to the table.

One night after dinner he spoke matter-of-factly. "I think it's time."

"Time?"

"Time I stopped driving. It's not safe anymore."

I may have known it had to happen, but I wasn't prepared for the finality of it. The symbol of independence he so eagerly grasped as a teenager was gone forever. The one who taught me to drive would now depend on me for transportation. Momentary sadness tugged at my heart and threatened to explode in my throat.

◆ ◆ ◆

The Merediths were Bob's neighbors. Sort of eccentric, definitely reclusive. Things went into the house and never seemed to come out. Even newspapers were kept, stacked high, creating walls against walls. Bob used to speculate that if they were to die in the house, it could be months before anyone found them. Among Mr. Meredith's prized possessions was a 1939 Nash. He would back it out of the garage on Sunday and take Mrs. Meredith for a drive. Except for shopping trips, that was about all the use the car got. After eleven years Mr. Meredith bought a new car. Knowing that Bob had to be close to driving age, he asked Bob Senior if Bob Junior would like to buy his Nash.

Bottom line: before Bob had his license to drive, he bought his first car. He was elated. He would have scrubbed floors to pay for it. In fact, he did, working as a janitor after school to earn the money. We were dating at the time, but if for some reason I had said, "It's me or the car," the car would have won hands down.

The day he turned seventeen, the buzzer sounded on our apartment intercom.

I hurried into the kitchen and picked up the earpiece. "Yes?"

"Hey! Look out the front window!"

The speaker went silent. I hung up the intercom and hurried to the front window. From our sixth-floor apartment

I could see Bob standing on the street below, wearing his leather aviator jacket. He waved excitedly at me. I hoisted open the window.

"What are you doing?" I yelled.

"Look!" He waved a small piece of paper. "I got my license!" He pointed toward the car, the pride of his life. "Want to go for a ride?"

A split second passed while I considered the consequences of unfinished homework and missed practicing.

"I'll be right down."

On the other hand, when I hit the legal driving age of seventeen, my father refused to teach me. His exact words: "I am not going to be responsible for putting another woman driver on the road." Clearly, in his eyes, this was a male realm, and all my begging and pleading fell on deaf ears. When Bob and I married I still did not know how to drive. Bob took it upon himself to teach me.

Perhaps this is the place to examine the instinctive bond between man and machine. Males, in general, have a love affair with cars. It is intense and apparently genetic. When David was first able to grasp a block it became a car, complete with motor sounds. It sped across the tray on his highchair and screeched to a halt at make believe stop signs.

His first sentence consisted of two words: "Car go." At naptime his bed was always filled with cars. As he drifted off to sleep you could hear little-boy car noises giving life to the two-inch vehicles. When we went for a drive, he sat in his car seat and watched every move his daddy made.

As a youngster he would put Cleo, the ever-patient dog, in the back seat and "drive" the parked car to the beach. Like his father before him, when it came time to get his license he just knew how to drive. He passed the driving test with flying colors.

His first car, a pre-owned Firebird, was his pride and joy. I think he would have slept in it if we had given him permission. Although his belongings were frequently scattered about his room, the Firebird was immaculate. Washed and waxed until you could see your reflection. Once the neighbor remarked, "David, if you take half as good care of your wife as you do of that car she'll be a very lucky lady."

That said, we turn back to Bob attempting to teach me to drive, on a stick shift. About cars I knew two things: you put air in the tires and gas in the tank. With respect to the technique required to drive a car I knew even less: you put your feet on the pedals and your hands on the steering wheel.

We were married in August. One Saturday morning in September Bob asked, "How about a driving lesson today?"

"Okay. Do I need anything?"

"Like what?"

"Oh, I don't know. A license for me, a crash helmet for you."

He laughed. "Nah. You won't be doing any real driving. At least not on the road. We'll find an empty parking lot, and you can get the feel of the car."

We climbed into the car and he drove around until he spotted an almost empty motel parking lot. He pulled in and drove around to the side. After turning off the engine, he showed me where everything was and then told me to scoot over and he would get in the passenger seat.

Obediently I slide into the driver's seat. Problem. Bob was over six feet tall; I hit the charts at about five-three. My feet didn't even touch the pedals.

"Hmmm. There's a lever or bar or something under the front of the seat. See if you can find it."

I felt around. Nothing. By then, Bob was leaning over trying to find the release mechanism under the driver's seat.

"Well, it's got to have one."

With that he was out the door, around the car, opening the driver's door, and motioning me out. He bent down and looked under the front seat.

"Ah! Here it is."

With one hand he released the lever. With the other hand behind the seat he tried to push it forward. It didn't budge.

"Tell ya' what. You get in the seat and, when I pull the lever, try to move it forward. Okay?"

"Yeah, sure. How do I do that?"

"Just scrunch forward with your legs and tush."

I climbed into the seat, stepping on Bob's hand in the process.

"Oh! I'm sorry! Are you okay?"

"Just a terminal wound. Not to worry."

After much jockeying with the seat, we finally got it where I could depress the gas pedal. Bob returned to the passenger seat.

"Okay. Now step on the clutch."

I remembered the name, after all he had just told me. But there were three pedals, and I wasn't sure which was which. "Which one is the clutch?"

His look said, "How could you live for twenty-one years and not know which one is the clutch?"

Not only did he have to explain that again, but I was never able to grasp "let the clutch out a little." Not enough, and you grind the gears. Too much, and the car stalls. To top it off, even with the seat forward as far as it would go, I could not completely engage the brake pedal.

Finally Bob said, "Look, maybe it will all make sense if you start it up and drive around the parking lot."

Why not? I put the key in the ignition and turned it.

Nothing.

"You have to give it some gas."

I tried again. This time I stepped on the gas. The engine roared into life, and I do mean ROARED.

"Too much! Not so much gas!"

I let up on the pedal, and the car purred softly. Slowly the car rolled forward. I won't go into all the details, but as the car hiccupped around the corner of the motel, Bob said, "Now shift into second."

I ground my way into second and the car began to buck.

"Gas! Gas! Give it more gas!"

I pressed down on the gas pedal. The car surged forward and landed on the front lawn of the motel. The motel door flew open and a man came running out.

"What are you doing?" he bellowed.

By now Bob was out of the car.

"I'm sorry. I'm trying to teach my wife to drive," he muttered, as he shook his head from side to side

"Oh. Lots o' luck. Be careful getting that thing off my grass."

Bob opened the driver's door. I was already in the passenger seat. Without a word he maneuvered the car off the grass and we headed for home. Nine summers would come and go without another lesson. Only after the purchase of an automatic did he feel brave enough to try again.

◆ ◆ ◆

The elephant in the tea seemed to have taken up permanent residence in my throat. I stretched out my arms, palms up, and with a smile on the outside, said, "Your taxi awaits." I leaned across the table and planted a kiss on Bob's cheek.

Little by little the disease was consuming him. There was no point in keeping score. It always ended the same way: another point for ALS, zero for Bob.

Chinwok sat in the driveway, unused.

"I'd like to go sit in it, but I'm not sure I can get in."

"Oh, sure. I'll be right there to give you a boost." Why did I say things like that? Anyone who has been in a motorhome built on a truck chassis knows that the step up into it is substantial. There are grab bars beside the door to give you something to grasp, but Bob was not able to use his hands. There was no way I could catch him if he started to fall. I went into the kitchen, snatched up the small step-stool, carried it outside, and set it on the driveway in front of the open door of the motorhome.

"Don't worry. I'll stand behind you." Oh, yeah. And get crushed like a bug if he falls.

He wobbled up the step and inside. I opened the windows, and we sat at the table.

"Would you like some iced tea?"

"Umm. That'd be kind of nice."

I went back into the house and got two glasses of tea and a straw for Bob. We sipped our tea in the pleasant breeze that blew through the RV's window. Neither of us spoke. It was a moment heavy with nostalgia. Finally I reached across the table and touched his hand.

"A lot of memories," I spoke quietly.

His deep pools of blue glistened as he stared out the window. He nodded. Then he turned to me and, in his take-charge voice, said, "Time to get out of here."

Right. I hadn't thought about getting him out, only getting in. I stood at the bottom of the step as Bob hovered in the doorway. Later I would learn that Carl, a neighbor, was watching from his kitchen window as the little drama unfolded.

"I can't do this."

"Yes you can."

"What? Do you think you're going to catch me if I fall?"

"You're not going to fall."

There is so much we take for granted about the way our bodies move. Now, with his shoulder and upper-arm muscles unable to help, keeping his body upright while stepping out into space was intimidating. For five minutes, he stood in the doorway while I cajoled, pleaded, and encouraged. Finally he stepped off and tottered to the driveway. I put my hand out to steady him as he staggered. We walked into the house in silence.

He never set foot in Chinwok again.

Each day when I drove Bob to work, I left him in compassionate, caring hands. Patricia, his right-hand at work, now became his hands, literally. After the initial shock subsided, she sought ways to make his life easier by attending an ALS support group. This was not part of her job description, but she accepted it without a word of protest. She never complained about the extra load. With businesslike demeanor she got Bob ready for the day ahead: telephone headset, foot-operated dictating machine, a straw in his coffee with the cup placed close enough for his mouth to reach when he bent over.

In addition to all the usual secretarial duties, she watched over him like a mother hen. Fetched out-of-reach documents, cleaned his glasses, wiped his nose, scratched an itch caused by an errant hair, and clucked if I was late to pick him up. One of the doctors at Henry Ford suggested Bob retire and spend "the good months left" traveling or doing something he enjoyed. Bob wouldn't even consider the suggestion. "I can't think of anything I'd rather do. My work is as much a part of me as breathing and, until that breath is gone, I'll keep doing it."

Patricia made it possible. Without her help he couldn't have continued.

We are all gifted differently. Now, the "gift" Bob had of dealing with an issue, putting it behind him, and moving on would see him through. The attribute I had once viewed as a liability would prove to be a plus.

This was the way things were.

Yearning for what was lost wouldn't help.

Feeling sorry for yourself was pointless.

Move on.

No despair.

No pity.

CHAPTER 12

*I*n late September we attended the regional convention of National Religious Broadcasters. The Board of Directors, aware of Bob's battle with Lou Gehrig's disease, planned to use the occasion to recognize his four decades in broadcasting. Bob was notified ahead of time.

As I drove into LA for the meetings, he remarked, "You know, when you get an award because you've done something for a long time, it's usually for one of the following reasons: you're very old, you're very sick, or you're dead."

I smiled. "Well, it's not the first and certainly not the last. I suppose that means it's the middle one, but you don't look sick nor do you act it."

"Yeah. Funny disease, isn't it? But we'll keep things normal as long as possible."

Like most conventions, this one began with initial schmoozing, greeting old friends, and milling about making nice. People tend to be uncomfortable around someone with an incurable disease, unsure of how to act or what to say. Most people expected Bob to look sick—thin, haggard, gray, or to be in a wheelchair. Except for the wasting of his left arm, which now hung uselessly from his shoulder, Bob looked great. Totally normal.

The initial awkwardness quickly abated when Bob readily

expressed acceptance of his condition. We visited. We laughed. We listened. There were even unexpected smidgens of humor we squirreled away to be recalled on a dismal day.

Maryann walked by and upon seeing Bob greeted him warmly and gave him a hug. Having no control over his left arm, it swung around and landed on her backside. This well-endowed spinster recoiled in surprise and stammered, "I—I have to see someone." She hurried away.

"Where did Maryann go in such a hurry?" I asked.

With a look of chagrin, he replied, "I don't think she knows. My hand landed on her tush, and she probably thinks I'm a dirty old man. Maybe you better tell her."

I tried to keep the laughter from bubbling up as I reached for his shoulder. "Goodness! I can't leave you alone for a minute!" By this time we were both trying to contain the laughter. "I'm sure she'll find out."

Later in the day she sought him out, clearly distressed over hearing the news of his condition. In a reversal of roles, Bob became the giver of comfort.

And then there was Herb. "BOB," he spoke slowly and deliberately in a voice twenty decibels above normal. "HOW—ARE—YOU—DOING? IT'S—GOOD—TO—SEE—YOU—LOOKING—SO—WELL."

"Good to see you too, Herb."

"I'LL—BE—PRAYING—FOR—YOU."

"Well, thank you. That's very kind."

This pudgy little man with gray hair, wearing a gray suit, stood there awkwardly shifting from one foot to the other, and then with the same precise articulation loudly announced, "I'LL—BE—GOING—NOW."

As he left the room, Bob raised his eyebrows and whispered, "I'm not deaf."

We both started to laugh.

Scattered among the light-hearted camaraderie was the isolated somber moment. When a colleague questioned the Almighty's actions, Bob was the voice of reason. "God's not wringing His hands, surprised at what has happened. He's still in control."

"Yeah, well, when I get to heaven I'm going to ask Him a thing or two."

With a rueful smile Bob replied, "When you get to heaven, you'll be so overwhelmed by the holiness and majesty of God you won't even remember this."

"Yeah, well, maybe so, but it seems so unfair."

"You know, life's not fair. If it were we'd all be born with a high IQ and a full head of thick, naturally curly hair." Laughter lifted the heavy moment.

Only a handful were aware of the disabling progress of the disease. When he was called up to the platform to accept the award, I experienced a momentary panic. I wasn't worried about him walking, but would he be able to carry the plaque? Not with his left hand. Was there enough strength in the right?

I leaned over and whispered, "Want me to come with you?"

He shook his head.

I didn't breathe as he made his way to the front.

Bob clutched the award with his right hand and stood listening to the words and applause that followed. I watched the plaque begin to list ever so slightly, *Oh please! Somebody help him!* And then he was making his way back to the table. I could tell by the way he gripped the award that every muscle in his body tensed to keep from dropping it. As he neared the table, I reached for the plaque. It fell into my hands.

My eyes misted.

He had done it.

Alone.

I adored him.

I was so proud of him at that moment, not for forty years in broadcasting, but for the sixty-second journey he had just made to the platform and back. I joined in the applause that swelled around him.

The fingers of Bob's right hand had movement but not much strength. He could grip or carry things, but the action required enormous effort and faded rapidly. Lifting his hand above the elbow, a movement dependent on muscles of the arm, was almost impossible.

His legs appeared unaffected, but one night, walking from the bathroom towards the bed, he fell. His leg just buckled. It seemed to happen in slow motion. Even as I yelled his name, I grabbed for his torso to cushion the fall. We landed next to the bed.

Remembering the scene months earlier with the bionic chair, we managed to wriggle his frame up onto the bed. We sat on the edge of the bed, exhausted, shaken, subdued. Was this the start of diminishing strength in his legs?

We thought we knew the enemy. In reality we were clueless. He needed my help with all the "routines of daily living." The words I read earlier in the medical reference books were just that, words. Like growing up in Nebraska and reading about the ocean and seeing pictures of it, and then visiting the gleaming sandy beaches of New Jersey and being struck dumb by the pure vastness of the ocean. Or learning about the pyramids in Egypt, and listening to people speak eloquently about theories of construction and then finally setting foot on the sands of the desert and gazing at them in person. Overwhelming.

◆　◆　◆

I heard the garage door open and a few seconds later the sound of footsteps as Bob took the stairs two at a time.

"How much do you love me?" he queried, coming into the kitchen. I could tell by the grin on his face he was bursting with exciting news.

"Hmmm," I began, pretending I was trying to figure it out, "let's see." I pondered the question, furrowing my brow. "From the fencepost to 'Newgene' in Oregon." I smiled, recalling the expression David coined when he was two.

Bob gave me a hug. "Congratulations! You have just won the grand prize! An all expense paid trip to Israel and the Middle East!"

"No kidding! Are we really going?"

"Yep. Here's the itinerary." He snagged a sheet of paper from his breast pocket. "We leave in six weeks. Jordan, Israel, Egypt."

"Six weeks! We don't even have passports!"

"Never fear, Bob the magnificent will make it all come to pass." He grinned. "Seriously, that darkroom we built downstairs is going to be really productive. Now, go change, I'll take some pictures, and you can choose the one you like best. I'll Fed-Ex them and the information to Seattle tomorrow."

Six weeks later we flew into JFK and landed in a raging snowstorm. One by one our group gathered, only to be informed the flight was delayed due to weather.

We waited.

The storm grew worse.

And waited.

Snow piled up.

And waited.

By the time the airport closed and grounded all flights, it was too late to snag one of the adjacent hotel rooms. We were stuck in the airport with hundreds of unhappy campers.

Bob looked around the holding area. "Looks like we're here for the night. Let's grab a couple of those chair cushions and try to get some zzz's."

Typical reaction. If you can't change the circumstances, roll with them. Meteorological records would look back on this night and the next day as a fluke–the storm that brought the city to a standstill. What we hadn't considered was that while we were enjoying the lodging and culinary delights of the airport–cushions on the floor and chips out of a vending machine–our tour guide was frantically trying to reschedule us. We were two days behind. Every hotel, every meal, every interview, as well as transportation had to be rebooked not just for two people, but a group of fifty. As a result, the original agenda was moot. It was plan as you go. Two days later we began our trip.

Part of the tour included Egypt, land of the Pharaohs. We were scheduled to fly into Cairo, but accommodations for that part of the trip were so messed up by the delay in New York that instead of flying from Jerusalem to Cairo we were bussed across the Sinai and ended up in Giza.

We arrived in the dark of night. As the bellboy carried our bags to the room I asked, "Can you see the pyramids from here?"

"Oh, yes. Just look out the window in the morning."

We were both exhausted and fell into bed and a sound sleep. At first light I slipped quietly out of bed and pulled open the drapes. An involuntary gasp escaped my lips. There before me, almost within reach, the pyramids rose from the desert sand. Stunned, I sank to the floor and stared at them in silence. There was nothing blocking the view between our motel and the ancient wonders.

"Can you see the pyramids?" a sleepy voice rose from the heap of covers.

I nodded, struck mute by the spectacle.

Bob stumbled out of bed and stood beside me. "Oh, my goodness," he breathed. Kneeling on the floor behind me, he slipped his arms around me. "Did you ever in your wildest dreams think we'd see the pyramids of Egypt? I mean, really see them? In person?" He hugged me close.

I could only shake my head. They were majestic. All the books and TV programs that tried to explain how they were built before modern technology seemed insignificant. They were there. Great monoliths. Overpowering. Overwhelming.

◆   ◆   ◆

Even with the pictures Bob took, there was no way to do justice to those magnificent structures. And, even though you could paint pictures with words, there weren't enough adjectives to describe what we had seen in person.

Now we found ourselves putting feet to the words, "routines of daily living." There are personal care rituals we do every day. We've done them for so many years we don't think about them—we just do them. Like showering. We worked out our own routine. I showered, then Bob got in the shower with me. I washed his hair, made sure he was clean, then got out and dried off, while he stayed under the spray of warm water. Wrapped in a towel, I reached in, turned off the water, helped him out, and dried him off.

"You never get my eyes dry," he complained after about the third or fourth day, "It feels really uncomfortable." I began to pay attention to what I did for myself. I discovered I was being too gentle with him.

The counter-height stool from the kitchen got moved into the bathroom, and he perched on it while I shaved his face and combed his hair. Gone was the hair cross-over-do. Susan, the perpetually bubbly hairstylist, cut his hair and combed it straight back. Frankly, it looked better.

I stood by as he hovered low over the sink to use the electric toothbrush he could still hold. He tried to help with dressing, but I buttoned his shirt, tucked it in, zipped his fly, put on his shoes and socks, and tied his shoelaces. I cut his fingernails and toenails, a job I disliked and he dreaded. We readily turned that chore over to a podiatrist recommended by Dr. Hedstrom—the only personal care routine we relinquished to someone outside the family.

And then there was eating. We tend to graze on and off all day and never pause to think about the muscles involved. I marveled at the complexities of the human body we take for granted. Eating now seemed like a small miracle; truly a gift from God.

Just for Bob to get the food to his mouth became a personal battle to retain some semblance of independence. He bent lower and lower over the plate as the meal progressed until finally surrendering to the fatigue and accepting my offer to help him finish. Once, in frustration, he emitted a guttural roar. A sound that came from somewhere deep within his soul. A sound so intense that I startled.

This was more than a disease; it was a creeping dread. Bob could no longer be alone. At work or at home someone had to be with him or within calling distance every minute. How did people manage who lived alone? Impossible.

We counted the days until Carolyn would arrive.

The ALS Clinic at Henry Ford sent the results of their findings to Dr. Hedstrom and referred us to the Neuromuscular Center at USC. With a summer free from the regimen of doctor's appointments now behind us, we made our first contact with USC. They asked us to bring all Bob's previous records. I wasn't too anxious to see Dr. Baxter since our final encounter had been both caustic and abrupt, so I waited until his day off before I called the office. His receptionist answered.

"Hi Jennifer. This is Barbara Ball."

"Well, hi. I haven't seen you in a while. How's Mr. Ball doing?" They had established a bond and the genuine warmth in her voice reached over the telephone.

"That's why I'm calling. He has an appointment at USC. They need a copy of his records. If I stopped by this afternoon could you have them ready for me?"

"Oh, sure. Make it after two o'clock, okay?"

At 2:45 I walked into the empty waiting room. As promised, Jennifer had a packet of papers waiting for me. She had copied Bob's medical records, as well as all of the notes and comments she found in the folder. That's how we happened to have copies of Baxter's analysis after each appointment.

"You been on vacation?" she asked, and without pausing for an answer continued, "I've missed you. Is Mr. Ball doing better?"

I suddenly realized she didn't know. Either Baxter hadn't put the report in Bob's folder or she hadn't read it.

"He's been diagnosed with ALS."

"Oh no! I'm so sorry." Tears filled her eyes. "Sometimes I hate this job. Wait there a minute." She got up from the desk and a moment later appeared beside me in the waiting room. She threw her arms around me. "I'm glad I got to know him. If I can do anything to help, please call."

On the day of Bob's appointment at USC, I parked in the handicapped space in front of the clinic. The weakness in his legs had curtailed any prolonged walking. The shorter, the safer. I hung the disability placard from the rearview mirror and turned to Bob. "Ready?"

"You really think we need to park here?"

"Hmmm." I nodded. "Too much concrete. Too many curbs. I don't want to take any chances."

I walked around and helped him out of the car.

Once again, we filled out multiple forms, described the onset of the disease, and verbally relived the past twenty months. Bob was questioned, poked, prodded, and subjected to multiple lab tests. One thing was different; we met Rita.

"Mr. Ball? I'm Rita. I'm part of the MDA clinic team. I'll be working with you to see that you stay ahead of this disease."

I'm sure someone told us that the ALS clinic was sponsored by MDA, the Muscular Dystrophy Association, but like so much of the information that bombarded us after the diagnosis, it had not registered.

"I don't understand. Why is MDA involved?"

"ALS is one of the many neurological diseases under the umbrella of MDA."

"What exactly is your role?" I asked.

"Any equipment prescribed by the clinic, from a wheelchair to a hospital bed, will be backed by MDA. Your insurance will be billed first, but if they won't pay the entire amount, MDA will guarantee the difference. That means there's no waiting. The provider can fill the order at once without having to contact the insurance company and wait for an okay."

In the long run, Bob's insurance covered all the medical equipment, but the awareness that another resource could be tapped eased his financial concerns. Money or not, we would have been lost without Rita.

Unlike paralysis, ALS is not static. It is continually progressing, continually getting worse. You must make constant adjustments, and if you don't prepare ahead of time it's too late. Like the episode with the signature stamps. Whereas we didn't know what was coming next, Rita had been through this before. She knew what to expect. She kept prodding us to prepare for the next loss before it showed up. She became a friend, a mentor, someone who understood.

Most family doctors never see an ALS patient. They read about the disease and perhaps get a glimpse of someone with ALS warehoused in a hospital bed. The GP shuffles the patient off to the neurologist, who understands the clinical aspect of the disease but not the patient. Here we were surrounded by people whose entire focus was the ALS patient. We breathed a sigh of relief.

As we completed that first appointment the neurologist said, "We'd like to schedule you for a muscle biopsy."

"I've already been diagnosed with ALS. Why do you need a muscle biopsy?"

"For confirmation and research purposes. This is strictly voluntary, but we'd appreciate it if you would do this. Just a small sliver from your thigh. We'll do it right here in the office."

The next day we returned for the biopsy.

Bob walked in the door.

He left in a wheelchair.

I helped him into the passenger seat, collapsed the chair, and opened the rear door to stow it. An elephant sat in the back seat.

CHAPTER 13

$\mathcal{C}$arolyn arrived with her car packed to the roof. The rest of her belongings, whatever UPS couldn't handle, left behind.

Friends left behind.

Business left behind.

The life she knew left behind.

Would she ever get it back?

Somehow it didn't seem fair. Just because she was single and childless, the burden of helping Mom care for Dad fell on her shoulders. More than a child should have to sacrifice for a parent. Wrapped in our own losing battle, we sometimes forgot she too battled the grief of impending loss. In spite of the circumstance, from day one the *joie de vivre* she brought with her would never flag. Even on the most desolate of days, there would be a smile on her face and a lilt in her voice.

Days after she arrived, David flew down from Seattle and drove away with my car.

We no longer needed two.

The door slammed shut.

End of an era.

The exodus from the ALS Clinic in the loaner wheelchair was only a precautionary measure. A few weeks later, however, as we walked the corridor of a local hospital to visit a friend, Bob stumbled. I grabbed for his belt.

"Can you do this?"

"It's only a couple more doors. I'm okay."

On the way back to the parking lot, the strain was visible. His legs leaden. His feet heavy. He did not speak. The task of putting one foot in front of the other consumed him completely. By the time we got to the car and I helped him into the passenger seat, he was exhausted. That was the last long walk.

Walk about the room? Yes. But each morning we would park the car in the handicapped spot outside the office building, haul out the wheelchair compactly stored behind the front seat, help him out of the car into the wheelchair, and push it down the hallway, into the elevator and into the office. No longer could he make the trek on his own or with someone at his side.

Our neighborhood was congenial but, with six-foot fences surrounding each property, not terribly social. There was no possibility of chitchat over the back fence. Most of the households were made up of working couples. When they came home, dog-tired, they wanted their privacy. On weekends they enjoyed their toys: boats, ski-doos, RVs, and motorcycles, or going to the mall and spending the money they'd just earned. They seemed to fit the California stereotype: "work hard, play hard."

Carl lived across the street. Retired at the young age of fifty-five, he puttered around the house and yard each day, while his wife continued to work. On this sunny morning he was outside working in his front yard. We knew each other by name, exchanged pleasantries, waved and smiled, and that was about it. I hesitated before crossing the street. If we needed help someday I might not have time to explain why. He had to be told.

"Hi, Carl!" I called as I crossed the street. "How you been doing?"

"Oh, just fine. Haven't talked to you in a long while. Everything okay at your place?"

"Well, not exactly. I'm sure you've witnessed some coming and going around the place." I looked away, finding it difficult to know how to proceed. "I thought I better let you know what's going on. Bob's been diagnosed with ALS, Lou Gehrig's disease."

"Oh, no!" There was a mixture of horror and compassion on his face. "I saw you trying to coax him out of the motorhome a couple of weeks ago." He shook his head, "I thought he was drunk. Why didn't you ask for help? Why didn't you tell me?"

I screwed up my face. "It's really hard to tell other people."

"Oh, Barbara! That's what neighbors are for, to help each other." He shook his head again. "Do you have any help?"

"Our daughter, Carolyn, has moved back home to help. You've probably seen her zipping around in that little Mazda."

He grimaced and shook his head again. "Just shows how wrong you can be. I figured she got divorced or broke up with someone and came home—you know how kids are today. I don't know an awful lot about Lou Gehrig's but I know it's nasty."

"It is. Bob's lost the use of his arms and hands, and his legs are getting weak."

"Is he still able to work?"

"Still putting in a full day. The office staff has been great, and his secretary is terrific."

He sighed deeply, "Now listen, anytime you need help please call. I mean it. Anytime. Day or night."

"Thanks Carl."

By the middle of December, words we did not know or had only heard in passing became part of our vocabulary. Everyday speech was peppered with terms like muscle atrophy, muscle wasting, range of motion, and the ever-present fasciculations. We now knew what durable medical equipment meant, and it seemed as if every week we added more of it. A shower chair and a raised toilet seat. Mobile arm supports and a docking station. I thought a docking station had to do with the space program. Maybe it does, but it's also a place to park a mouth-stick—another new word.

I began to feel like Alice in Wonderland.

We were in a strange place where nothing was as it should be.

And there was more to come.

Without the use of his arms, Bob couldn't raise himself up. The clinic approved a hospital bed. "An electric one," said Rita. "You can raise the head up and swing his legs over the edge. It will make it easier on your back when you get him out of bed."

Years earlier we purchased a king-sized bed. Not the standard king. A king-sized headboard with twin beds attached. The beds could be clamped together but, when unclamped, parted easily to change the fitted twin sheets. A king-size top sheet and bedding covered the whole thing. The day the hospital bed arrived, the delivery man helped move out one twin bed and replace it with the hospital bed. It fit the space perfectly. When made up with the king sheet and quilt, it looked like our regular king bed. That's what Bob wanted. Everything kept as normal as possible. He was pleased. I could still be at his side.

The first night, however, was anything but pleasant. Bob was accustomed to a firm mattress. We'd specified a firm mattress and supposedly that's what we got.

"That was like sleeping on a bowl of oatmeal mush," he commented the next morning, "If this is supposed to be firm, I hate to think what soft must be like. Can we put a board under it or something?"

"Something. I'll figure it out while you're at work."

A good night of sleep was a must. He had to have something firmer than the sagging wire springs that supported the mattress.

Carolyn helped me move the mattress off the bed and set the old bed-board on top of the springs. With the mattress back in place, I pushed the button to raise the head. The board and mattress shot straight up.

"You planning on launching him?" she giggled.

A regular bed-board wouldn't work.

I left for the lumberyard and returned with a dozen one-by-twos cut into thirty-nine inch lengths and a roll of replacement webbing for lawn chairs. To be honest I really wasn't sure what I was doing, but I visualized something that could move with the bed. If the slats were placed about one-half inch apart, they would support the mattress and ride with the bed as it was raised or lowered. Something had to keep them from tumbling or sliding off—that's where the webbing came in. I put the boards on the bed to see if it would work.

"Uh-oh."

"What's the matter?" Carolyn asked.

"They're too long."

"What's too long?"

"The slats. This bed must be narrower than a standard twin. I should have measured it first," I answered as I hunted for the tape measure in the drawer of my sewing machine. "Oh, bother! It's only thirty-five inches."

"I'll get the saw," Carolyn commented, already on her way to the garage.

I marked each board at thirty-four inches. Finished, I was just about to go after her when she walked into the room.

"Will this do?"

"No. That's a metal saw." It suddenly occurred to me that we might not even have a saw. Bob was not exactly a handyman. Ask him to fix anything electronic—done. Develop and print pictures in the darkroom—a wizard. But put up a shelf? Forget it.

I followed Carolyn out to the garage. There was one handsaw in the toolbox; that would take forever. I was beginning to think I'd have to make a trip back to the lumberyard when I spotted the chainsaw hanging on the wall. It was small and electric.

"Perfect!"

"Mom! That's a chainsaw. It'll tear the wood apart!"

"Nobody's gonna' see it."

"And where do you think you're going to cut those boards? We don't have a workbench."

"Hmmm. I'll lower the hospital bed, hang the board over the edge, kneel on it and have at it. You may have to sit on the boards."

"Have you taken leave of your senses?"

"Probably."

In the end, the boards, interwoven in lattice-like fashion with the webbing and secured to the springs at the head of the bed, worked beautifully; shifting easily under the mattress as the bed was raised or lowered. The room, however, strewn with sawdust and wood chips, looked as if a crazed beaver had gotten loose. Or perhaps a neophyte cook with a hand-mixer.

◆ ◆ ◆

It was July. Hot. When you're eight months pregnant, heat is exhausting.

"I think I'll lie down for a while."

"Good idea. I'll make us something cool."

I frowned. "Make something? Like, in the kitchen?" I looked at him doubtfully.

He let out a laugh. "You don't think I can. I'll be fine." He pushed me towards the bedroom and added, "Go, Chubby."

"Ha, ha."

"I'll fix us some nice cool Jell-O. Is there any of that whipping cream left?"

"I think there's still some in the fridge. I'm not sure."

I walked into the bedroom shaking my head. This was a man who forgot how to operate a can-opener the day he said, "I do." But what could possibly go wrong with Jell-O?

This was the era of "cooking" with gelatin. You could do anything with it. Every week a new recipe appeared. Molded salads with chopped celery and shredded carrots or mandarin oranges and marshmallows. Main courses with chunks of chicken, sliced almonds, and broccoli encased in lemon-flavored Jell-O. Desserts? Serve it plain or fold in fresh fruit. Add a dollop of whipped cream and, *voila*, a dessert with no cooking involved. A couple of times I'd served it whipped: soft-set and whipped with an electric hand-mixer. It was cool and refreshing, and if you folded in some whipped cream it had the consistency of something more substantial.

Bob searched in the cupboard. *Ah, Strawberry Jell-O.* He read the instructions on the side of the box. Hmmm. Couldn't be too hard. He dumped the Jell-O in a bowl and put the kettle on to boil. When the kettle whistled, he pulled it off and set it on another burner. He read the instructions again and began to hunt for a measuring cup. He had no idea where to look. Afraid that the water might be getting cool, he grabbed a teacup, filled it with the hot water, and dumped it on the Jell-O. Then he read the instructions again and stirred it until the crystals dissolved.

Almost as an afterthought he read the "Quick Set" directions. *Oh, yeah, the quicker, the better.* Taking a tray of ice cubes out of the freezer compartment, he filled the teacup to overflowing with ice cubes and dumped them into the hot mixture. After a couple minutes of stirring, he popped it in the refrigerator. Satisfied with his culinary achievement, he sat in front of the fan and leafed through his current photography magazine.

After about half-an-hour he got up to check on the Jell-O. Stiff. Good job, he thought as he removed the bowl from the refrigerator and got the hand-mixer and beaters out of the drawer.

The sound of someone yelling "Oh, no!" jarred me out of my cozy cocoon of half-sleep. Shuffling down the hall, I glimpsed Bob, mixer in hand, with a look of utter dismay on his face. It took a second or two to take in the scene before me. There was red Jell-O everywhere. Chunks of Jell-O littered the counter. It hung from the cabinets. Sparkling red bits clung to the window and the light fixture. There was Jell-O on the floor rapidly being consumed by Skipper, the ever-hungry dog. The more I looked, the more I saw. The ceiling was speckled with it. It reached into the dining area and dotted the door to the laundry room. The only place that seemed to be devoid of Jell-O was the bowl.

I stared in disbelief. "What in the world happened?"

"I don't know. I was going to whip the Jell-O. I took it out of the fridge, stuck in the beaters and turned the mixer to whip. The next thing I know it's all over." He looked bewildered as he gazed at the ceiling.

For the first time, I noticed he, too, was covered with bits of red Jell-O. Blobs of the sticky stuff covered his clothes and nested in his hair. I began to laugh. From the incredulous look on Bob's face to the red-spattered kitchen, it was truly comical. "Poor, Honey." I grinned, "Working in the kitchen can be dangerous."

"I was only trying to please you," he muttered, his feelings hurt by my laughter. "I can't believe what a mess this is!"

"I love you for trying." I started to give him a hug, but stopped short unable to find a non-sticky spot. "Tell you what," I smiled. "I'll stay out of the darkroom; you stay out of the kitchen. How's that?"

Reluctantly he managed a sheepish smile, embarrassed that his culinary efforts had ended in such chaos.

"Help me clean up, and we'll go out later and get an ice cream cone."

With a dishpan of soapy water, we attacked the Jell-O. He cleaned the places I couldn't reach—both too high and too low. As we mopped up what was visible at first glance, we kept finding more. Just as we thought we found the last bit, one of us would gleefully shout, "Look! There's more!" We laughed hilariously over each new sighting.

After about twenty minutes of finding and rinsing, we thought we got it all; but for days afterward I found errant red stains here and there, and, when we moved six weeks later, I'm sure the new tenants found more.

It was a rather long time before Bob felt brave enough to try anything in the kitchen that vaguely resembled cooking.

◆ ◆ ◆

Any project takes twice as long as you think it should (isn't that one of Murphy's Laws?). If you don't have the proper tools, well, triple it. By the time Carolyn and I got the room cleaned up and the bed remade, it was time to pick up Bob. As we settled him into the car he asked, "So, what have you girls been up to this afternoon?"

We glanced at each other. "Oh, just trying not to mutilate each other."

On the next visit to the clinic, we were presented with a glimmer of hope. The most difficult thing surrounding a diagnosis of Lou Gehrig's is the knowledge that nothing can be done. No matter how hard you fight, you know you're going to lose. When the doctor said there appeared to be some success with Vitamin B shots, Bob agreed to try them.

"Have you ever given shots before?" The nurse looked at me as she asked the question.

I shook my head. "No."

"Well, you're going to learn," she said brightly.

"Right now?"

"Now. Make sure all the air is out of the syringe." She demonstrated by pushing the plunger all the way up. "Then fill it to this level." She turned the small bottle upside down, deftly inserted the needle, and slowly withdrew some of the liquid. "After you remove the needle, give it a thunk with your finger to get any air bubbles to the surface, then push out a drop to make sure there's no air in it. Now, pinch the muscle between your fingers, and plunge the needle in quickly."

I looked dubious.

"Have you ever played darts?"

I nodded.

"Just pretend it's a dart, and his muscle is the dart board." She smiled at Bob, "Once the needle is in, pull back gently on the syringe to make sure you haven't landed in a vein. If any red shows up in the syringe, you've hit a vein. In that case, withdraw the needle and try again. Okay. Your turn."

"Now?" I looked at her uneasily.

"Of course! Not gonna' turn you loose until I see you do it." She smiled.

"Shouldn't I practice on something besides my husband?"

"Not as long as I'm here. You'll do fine."

With the nurse supervising, I started with a fresh needle and gave Bob his first "B" shot. When I pinched the flesh on his upper arm, I couldn't help but notice how painfully thin his arms had become. For a moment my throat constricted. No giving in to the wave of sadness that welled up within me.

"How was that?" I asked him, then added, "I didn't feel a thing," and gave him a quick smooch on the cheek.

"Smart aleck," he said with a grin. The nurse laughed.

It was a Saturday. We were fixing lunch. Oh, let's clarify that. Carolyn was fixing lunch; I just cleaned up as she went along. She was an intuitive cook, with an uncanny sense of which herbs to use to awaken the flavor. Even a simple bowl of chili turned into something memorable at her touch. Made from scratch, with fresh tomatoes, cloves of fresh garlic, diced onions, and lots of pungent chili powder, the smell was enough to make you salivate long before it was ready. Finally, with a bowl of it under his nose, Bob would make little umming sounds as I spooned it into his mouth and remark, "You could sell this."

As we worked about the kitchen, the phone rang. From the one-sided conversation Bob could tell something devastating had happened. I hung up the receiver, crossed the room, and sat beside him on the couch.

"What is it?"

"That was Connie. Ted and Evelyn were killed in an accident yesterday."

A couple we knew from college days. Friends we had lived and worked with during the early years of our marriage. Our children were close in age and had often played together.

Carolyn, listening and watching, exclaimed, "Oh, no! That's awful. What happened?"

"A freak car accident. They were both killed instantly."

She turned back to the stove.

Bob, in a voice that was barely audible, whispered, "They're the lucky ones." His eyes met mine. In that unguarded moment, I caught a glimpse into his soul. Those tranquil pools of blue reflected the anguish within as he contemplated the ordeal that lay ahead. For an instant, I thought about loading him into the car and driving off a cliff. Instead, I put my arms around him and held him close.

When devastating events enter our lives, we can only rest in the assurance that God is Sovereign, in full control. Although we might be caught off-guard by the elephant in the tea, God is neither surprised nor dismayed by the events that have overtaken us. This knowledge alone would help Bob persevere and give me the strength to see him through.

CHAPTER 14

It was a Chamber of Commerce day. The sun glistened off the dew-speckled landscape. The flower bed surrounding me was a palette of vibrant color. With a trowel clutched in my hand, I gazed over the drift of blossoms. They seemed to spread to infinity.

"Bobbie."

The voice came from the gnarled apple tree. I looked up. "David, you little scamp! Come down from there, and don't call me Bobbie. I'm your mother."

"Bobbie."

The voice was real.

Forget flowers and apple trees. How long had Bob been saying my name?

"Ummm?" I questioned, rousing reluctantly from the clutches of the dream world.

"I'm stuck. I can't turn over."

He had enough muscle control left to "scrunch" a little and find a comfortable position, but, with his legs getting weaker and his arms unable to lend assistance, turning over was becoming more difficult. Now the electric blanket was too heavy for him to complete that simple maneuver. We needed something lightweight yet warm. The electric blanket would have to go, replaced by an ultra-lightweight down quilt.

Plenty warm for the hot-blooded Norwegian I married.

I was left with icy feet.

My body chemistry demanded warm feet before sleep would come. I tried wearing heavy socks. They provided some help, but not enough.

Carolyn went shopping and returned with a twin-sized electric mattress pad for my bed. Problem solved. I gained the needed warmth, and Bob slept through the night with only an occasional assist.

Rita was at it again. At our next visit, she recommended a wheelchair, not a loaner, but his own. "It's going to take several weeks. Time to get the ball rolling." She smiled. "No pun intended."

The doctor agreed. "We don't want you falling."

"Why does it take so long? Can't I just pick one out?" Bob asked.

They both looked slightly aghast at our ignorance. "No. You have to be fitted. It will be *your* chair. Custom-done to meet your needs. I'll have to write a prescription for you, and then everything has to clear with insurance."

As the doctor left to get his prescription pad, Rita motioned to us.

"Tell them you want a reclining wheelchair. A motorized one with arm supports," she whispered.

We looked at her blankly. Not a clue as to what she meant.

"Just do it," she said quietly.

Prescription in hand, we turned to Rita for clarification. "The reclining chair has a high back and a headrest. The entire back can be adjusted when, ah, it becomes necessary." She said the last part softly, almost with reluctance.

It took a second for the words to register. As I grasped the full meaning of her words, the color in the room faded to gray. Images of old men with heads lolling to one side flashed on and off in my head. Eventually Bob wouldn't be able to hold his own head up.

Margie had just given birth to number four. As our new

granddaughter gained motor skills, Bob was losing them. She was progressing, he was regressing. At what point would they pass each other? Bob's words replayed in my head: "You've got to be tough." The sound of Bob's voice broke through the fog.

"And motorized? Without the use of my hands, is it really practical?" Then almost as an afterthought, he murmured, "I suppose it would make it easier for Bobbie to push."

I still marvel at Rita's patience and persistence. She knew exactly what he needed. We knew squat. Obviously, we still had much to learn.

"It does come with an assistant control, but there are all kinds of controls available to operate a chair. You have to be evaluated to determine which muscles are still functioning. Most likely a chin control would work best for you. You also need to be fitted for the correct size chair, and someone will probably want to visit your home and check out the workplace."

And so Bob faced a new delegation of supporters. He was observed and measured, scrutinized and evaluated. And Rita was right, of course. The chin control was recommended. The final wording of the prescription read: "One motorized reclining wheelchair, rechargeable battery packs, arm supports, chin control."

When we eventually got the chair home, for the first time in months, Bob was able to move about the house and workplace by himself. At fifty-seven, he savored this small measure of autonomy as much as that first car at seventeen.

The home we left in Oregon was custom-built. A house built on a sloping lot, it had seven levels. Garage on the first level, two bedrooms, bath and laundry on the second level, large vaulted entry on the third level, living room on the fourth level, dining room and kitchen on the fifth level, another bedroom and family room on the sixth level, and on the seventh level a bridge over the vaulted entryway led to the master bedroom and bath. A fun house to live in. Kept us running up and down stairs all day. Good for a workout, but totally impractical for someone in a wheelchair.

When we moved to La-La Land, we were rattled by the cost of housing. We laughed in disbelief when the realtor showed us houses and quoted the asking price.

"You're kidding!"

"Nope. And it will probably be more next month."

A house in California cost twice as much as a similar one in Oregon.

I balked at the difference. Bob was insistent.

"We have to buy."

"But the real estate market is crazy!"

"That's the way it is. We just have to bite the bullet and carry a big mortgage."

Reluctantly I gave in. We bought with no idea that in four years Bob would be wheelchair dependent. We couldn't have chosen a more suitable house. Instead of seven levels, it was all on one level. The layout, with wide, short hallways and lots of open space, worked with us. The living room, dining room, family room, and kitchen all flowed into one another. Each area definitely separate, but open and airy. The durable medical equipment we would soon accumulate fit easily into the large master bedroom.

God alone knows the future. Looking at it from our current circumstance, could we doubt this was His provision? We could stay in our home. Changes would be minor.

"We're going to have to think about some remodeling."

Bob looked at me skeptically. "Like what?" he asked.

"A ramp at the front. I know it's only one step, but, ah, you're pretty big. And the shower needs to be redone. It's big enough, but we need better access, and a second showerhead would keep me warm while I'm bathing you."

"Bobbie, we have to be practical. My time is short. Whatever we can do to make things easier for you and Carrie is fine, as long as the house doesn't begin to look like a clinic. It already is starting to look that way," he added, referring to the equipment that was collecting in the bedroom.

The remodelers were great. Understanding we needed extra time in the morning, they worked around our schedule. When they finished, the concrete slope to the threshold had such a gradual incline that visitors didn't realize it was a ramp unless we brought it to their attention. The shower, big enough to start with, now included a second showerhead and an extra-wide door to accommodate a wheeled shower chair.

Bob was delighted with the additions.

He now turned his attention to computer software programs. He was on the hunt for a word processor that could be used by people with limited or no use of their upper extremities. Although voice recognition software was highly rated and the sample he received worked flawlessly, he immediately ruled it out.

"This is great software, and it would be super for right now. But then, what do I do when I start to lose the ability to speak and the program can't understand me? I'd have to get something else and start learning all over again."

I was in denial about that phase of the disease. The very idea of Bob not being able to speak was beyond imagination. The image of my claustrophobic, remarkably verbal love trapped in a body that could neither move nor speak was too appalling to even consider. His voice was his persona, his life, his livelihood.

◆ ◆ ◆

"Why are you going to Princeton?"

"It's close to home, and I plan on going into medicine," he answered with a shrug. "Be a doctor someday. My folks are pretty keen on the idea. You know: 'my son the doctor.' So, why are you going to Bob Jones?"

"That's where my sister goes, and Dad says he can send me there and not worry about what I'm up to."

"Aren't they kinda' strict?"

"Compared with a state school I suppose they are, but they can't possibly have as many rules as Daddy does!"

The wheels began to turn in his head. In a couple of months he had convinced his parents he should go to Bob Jones: "The first couple of years are pretty basic no matter where you go. I can take pre-med and then transfer later. The Christian values you've taught me will be reinforced." Years later he would tell me the real reason he went was because I was going and he was afraid to let me out of his sight.

Shortly after arriving on campus Bob was hired by the campus radio station. Assuming the role of an eager young reporter, when there was an accident on the highway in front of the school, Bob grabbed his press pass and a tape recorder and ran down to cover the pileup. It was bad. He turned pale, then nauseous, then faint. At that instant he changed his major from premed to radio broadcasting.

So long, M.D.

Hello, DJ.

He never looked back.

Bob fell in love with every phase of radio. Announcer. DJ. Sales. His bass voice flowed seamlessly over the airwaves as he made transitions appear effortless. Every afternoon he hosted a drive-time music program. Soon everybody on campus knew him by name. Heady stuff for a young kid. He was a BMOC (big man on campus). As Bob's recognition grew, so too did his perception of his own importance. Rules in the workplace did not apply to him. After all, he had a successful program, a great voice, and a great following.

But, the day of reckoning was coming.

One day the station manager, Jim Ryerson, called him in.

"This radio station is not dependent on you."

"What do you mean?"

"We don't need the 'Bob Ball' show."

"I'm just doing my job."

"Your ego is getting in the way of your performance."

"Who says?"

"You've got a bad attitude."

"But I don't think... "

"You're fired."

"But..."

"You're fired."

It was a defining moment, a kind of epiphany. It drove Bob to his knees. God had given him a deep mellow voice, and he couldn't take any credit for it. It was a humbling experience. An incident he would remember all his life. The next day he sought out Jim apologized and pleaded for his job back. Jim rehired him on the spot.

For the remainder of Bob's college years, Jim mentored him, encouraged him, prepared him for the world that lay beyond the college campus, and watched with a measure of satisfaction when Bob was hired by a CBS affiliate.

Few teachers make a lasting impact on our lives; those who hold our feet to the fire are the ones we recall with gratitude.

◆ ◆ ◆

Too soon the voice that had captivated me as a teenager, the voice Jim recognized for its potential, would be silent.

After researching and evaluating several software programs, Bob zeroed in on Words+ and its multiple components. With a feather-light trigger-switch that could be attached anywhere on his wheelchair, he could take advantage of any remaining usable muscle to operate the program. This first-rate software supported an augmentative communication program that would eventually be his voice.

To make use of the program, Bob needed a battery-operated portable computer with enough memory to run the software. Toshiba was highly recommended. He contacted the local Toshiba distributor and described the modifications he would need. Once again we found helpful, cooperative people responsive to Bob's needs and determined to meet them.

The call finally came that the Toshiba was ready. I parked the car outside the light industrial complex and walked into the building housing the company responsible for retrofitting the Toshiba for the end-user. Immediately the smell of perfume assailed my nostrils. The scent emanated from the blonde behind the desk in the small outer office. She barely looked up as she continued to file her nails.

"Yeah?" It was a question.

She was maybe thirty. Her blond hair was piled high on her head. The blouse she wore was low cut, brightly patterned, and clingy. The amount of makeup suggested it had been applied with a trowel.

"I'm here to see Mike," I volunteered.

She motioned towards a chair with her nail file and said, "Okay. Just wait." When she spoke her voice was nasal.

I sat. After about two minutes of filing and blowing, the front door opened and a young man carrying a briefcase walked in.

"Can I help you?" she purred.

The young man, apparently struck dumb by this vision of pulchritude, reached into his suit pocket, withdrew a business card, and handed it across the desk without a word.

Carefully moving the newly filed fingernails, she depressed the intercom button and announced, "Mr. Steffins, the Toe-she-bee man is here."

I clamped my lips together to keep from smiling and forced the bubbling laughter back down inside. I didn't dare look at the young salesman. Seldom do I make snap judgments about people, but in this situation I made an exception. Must have been her looks that got her this job or maybe she was a friend of someone in the company.

Eventually Mike came and led me into the backroom, where a small group of young techies were working on computers. He explained what had been done and showed me which cables went where. "And," he concluded, "you can use it like a regular computer if you decide you don't need all the extras."

As he boxed up the Toshiba I casually asked, "Is the girl at the front desk new?"

A hint of a smile played around his mouth before he responded. "No. Friend of the boss."

After a slight pause he added, "Sort of gives credence to all those blond jokes." He smiled broadly as he held the door open for me.

Near the end of January, we prepared for the annual trip to the National Religious Broadcaster's convention. We both knew that, short of a miracle, this would be the last convention Bob would attend. He looked forward to visiting with old friends. By now, most knew that he had ALS, but we would encounter those who had not heard and were visibly shaken to see him in a wheelchair.

Within the confines of the home or office, he felt secure enough to walk, but he couldn't possibly navigate the airport or the long hallways at the convention. Since his custom wheelchair had not yet arrived, we requested and received permission to take the loaner wheelchair out of state.

The first hurdle we encountered was the airport itself. The girl at the security checkpoint motioned for Carolyn and me to walk through the scanner and told Bob to go through the adjacent gate, which, of course, he could not do by himself.

"He can't maneuver the chair," I said, indicating the braces on his wrists.

"Oh. Well, leave him over there and get him when you are done." She nodded towards a fenced area.

With some apprehension I pushed Bob through the gate and left him sitting there, utterly helpless. I kept glancing over at him as we passed through the archway and then waited for the carry-on stuff to make it through the scanner. It seemed to take forever. Finally, with our goods in tow, we hurried over to get him.

A young man with a wand blocked our approach.

"You can't go this way."

"We have to retrieve that gentleman in the wheelchair," I replied, glancing over at Bob. He followed my gaze and seemingly for the first time noticed Bob and the chair.

"Oh. Okay. Stop back here and I'll clear him."

We stopped as instructed. The young man looked at Bob and said, "Just hold your arms out like this." He held his arms straight out like the wings of an airplane.

Trying hard to keep the smile off his face, Bob responded, "I don't think so."

The young man looked startled and then tried to recover his look of authority when I explained, "He can't move his arms."

"Oh, ah, ah." Clearly flustered, he continued, "Well, umm, ah, let's see "

"We can stand him up." Carolyn suggested.

"No!" he blurted out, probably envisioning a lawsuit if Bob were to fall. "Umm, could you hold his arms up for me?"

We ditched the carry-ons and lifted Bob's arms. Awkwardly, the attendant moved his wand down Bob's side, only to encounter a warning beep from the chair itself. At this point Carolyn again said, "We can stand him up."

"No, no, that's okay," he said quickly. Then with a shrug, he added, "Just go ahead."

When we finally got to the gate and settled into the lounge area, Carolyn looked at her daddy with wide-eyed innocence and, holding her arms straight out from the shoulders, said, "Hold your arms out just like this." The other people waiting for the plane must have wondered what we found so comical.

I can't say the trip was a piece of cake, but people were extraordinarily kind and helpful. During the convention we were directed through kitchens, in and out of service elevators, down deserted hallways and through doors marked "Do Not Enter." Aside from a few curious stares, nobody seemed to mind or question that we were off limits.

The first day we had a light breakfast sent up to the room. By noon Bob was famished. We stopped in the hotel dining area and ordered lunch.

After about three bites Bob said, "Stop doing that."

"What?" I asked.

"You open your mouth every time you put food in mine."

I'd probably been doing that for months, a carry-over from spooning food into the reluctant mouths of little children. I started to laugh. "Oh, Honey. I didn't realize I was doing that!"

"It's not funny," he said, deadly serious. Here, amidst his peers, the last thing he wanted was to be viewed with pity. What we did in private was one thing, but here in public he needed to retain a measure of dignity.

"I'm sorry, Hon, I really am," I said soberly. "If you catch me doing it again, just say my name to remind me."

I seldom glimpsed the emotional turmoil that hovered below the surface as he lost more and more control. As much as possible, we both fought to keep our emotions in check. We weren't trying to be stoic or brave, it was just too messy if we broke down. I had to wipe away his tears as well as mine and hold the hankie while he blew his nose, an undertaking he detested. It happened from time to time, and would happen again sooner than he expected.

We were late for the first general meeting.

We were late for everything.

Bob couldn't do anything to help get ready. I took care of his physical needs first then got him dressed for the day. His tie was the one thing that terrified me. I never got the hang of doing it correctly. On myself? No problem. But when I tried to fix it around his neck, the knot was too low or too tight, or the ends were grossly uneven. When David came down to pick up my car, he'd knotted a bunch of ties and loosened them for me so I could slip them over Bob's head and adjust the Windsor knot at his collar. I guarded those ties as if they were solid gold.

We wheeled into the meeting already underway, found two seats on the aisle about halfway down, and parked Bob's chair in the aisle. Almost as soon as we got settled, the houselights dimmed and Bob's face filled the screen above the platform. The voice of Al Sanders echoed through the convention hall.

"Robert Ball. What would NRB and, in fact, Christian radio be like without him? And this year Bob reaches a milestone—forty continuous years in broadcasting."

For more than ten minutes, Al traced Bob's life from infancy to his present battle with Lou Gehrig's. For weeks Al had secretly gathered photographs from family, even coming to the house while Bob was at work to make copies of pictures that hung on our walls. Now,

ELEPHANTS IN THE TEA

bigger than life, the pictures filled the hall. Pictures of his parents and sisters, of school days and marriage, and pictures of Bob with various presidents. Interspersed with sound bites from family and music arranged and performed by David, Al tied it all together with a cohesive flowing narrative.

What a treasure.

Taken by surprise, the tears flowed down Bob's face as one-by-one images of his children and grandchildren paraded across the screen.

I wiped his tears away.

I couldn't speak. The ever-present elephant lodged firmly in my throat as the flood of precious memories threatened to engulf us both.

CHAPTER 15

$\mathcal{T}$he worst of all scenarios.

On the flight home Bob began to sneeze.

By the time we pulled into the driveway, he had all the symptoms of a full-blown cold. We knew it was potentially serious. He'd been told, "Whatever you do, don't catch a cold. Your immune system is compromised, and the muscles that help keep your lungs clear are weak. You don't want pneumonia." After months of screening visitors to the house, we had turned him loose into the germ jungle. Contact with thousands of people at the hotel and then cooped up for hours in an airplane—the perfect breeding ground for an unwelcome bug.

Bob panicked.

We all panicked.

The doctor recommended some over-the-counter medication and cautioned me to watch for any signs the cold might be moving into his lungs.

Without the use of his hands, I had to wipe his nose or hold the tissue while he tried to clear stuffed passageways. For years you do this for a toddler as he angrily tries to pull away until, with much rejoicing, he finally gets the hang of it and does it himself. You never think you'll have to do it for an adult.

Bob was irritable and anxious. When Carolyn tried a little

light-hearted humor, he cut her off. We mirrored his attitude, talked in subdued tones, and tiptoed around. I know it was irrational, but I kept thinking I was somehow to blame.

For a week, a heavy cloud of discouragement hung over the house. Finally Bob showed signs of shaking it. The potential setback was past. We let out a collective sigh of relief and thanked God for bringing us through the crisis.

The prescription order for a motorized wheelchair had been submitted before we left for the convention, and it would be ready in a couple of weeks. We knew the chair would be too big and heavy to fit in the car. We needed a van.

In her typically helpful role, Rita provided us with a list of used vehicles already outfitted with a lift. When we checked out the list, two had already been sold, one had been used by a smoker (in such a confined space, the odor was overwhelming), and the owner of the last vehicle decided not to sell. Back to square one.

Everything was put on hold while Bob was under the weather. Now that he was beginning to feel better, we focused on the van. There was a measure of urgency involved since it was becoming more difficult to transfer him into the car. Getting him in the car, we ran the risk of dropping him; getting him out without whacking his head on the door frame was becoming a real backbreaker.

On Saturday morning we went hunting. Bob never even got out of the car at the first stop. When we pulled up beside the van, two salesmen immediately headed towards us.

"Uh-oh. Let's get out of here. I don't want to talk to anybody."

At the third or forth dealership, we spotted the vans at the back of the lot. "This looks safer. Maybe I can get out here and take a look."

I quickly got him into the wheelchair and pushed him over to the van. He peered into a conversion van with a raised roof. It was plush with upholstery. Even the walls and the ceiling were upholstered—charcoal gray. Once we had the van outfitted with a lift, his head would almost brush the ceiling.

"I don't like this at all! Too dark." Bob wrinkled up his nose. "Looks sort of like a coffin. I feel claustrophobic just looking at it."

"Nice van isn't it?" The voice came from behind. We hadn't seen him coming. "I'm Ralph." The salesman offered his hand. He was short and thin, with hair slicked across the top of his head. "Can I answer any questions for you?"

"No. We're just looking; trying to find out what's available." My hands stayed on the wheelchair as I started to push Bob towards our car.

"This is a real honey. It can easily be outfitted with hand controls."

It was an all too common conclusion: a man in a wheelchair, ergo his legs do not work but his hands do. As he continued to ramble on about the features of the van, I transferred Bob into the car, collapsed the wheelchair, stowed it in the back, and walked around to the driver's door.

"What color are you looking for?"

Oh, come on! "We're just looking today," I repeated as I started to get into the car.

"This is last year's model. I can give you a real deal. Here's my card."

Not wanting to appear heartless, I took the card and noticed that Ralph had scratched out the name of a previous salesman and written his name above it.

Oh, Lord. Forgive my impatience! Everybody has to make a living.

I conjured up a smile and hoped it appeared genuine. "Thank you, Ralph. If we come in again I'll ask for you." As we pulled away he was still talking. Maybe he still is.

We were suddenly aware of the challenging task we had before us. Each stop took longer than planned, and the salesmen tended to blather on and on about hand controls without pausing to ask what we needed.

As we drove towards home Bob remarked, "All the ones we've looked at are designed so I can't see out the window unless I bend my head down. What about a Vanagon? A pop-top? You know, a bus."

The irony of his suggestion struck me immediately. Our first new car was a Volkswagen. Would the last one be a Volkswagen? I kept the thought to myself. Whether Bob had the same thought I'll never know.

Just as the idea of a VW crept in, we became aware of an ad from Volkswagen picturing a van with a lift and offering a discount to anyone with a disability. That was the carrot. We'd get a light-filled van with windows all around, six inches of additional headroom, plus a refund to reduce the expense and installation of a lift. It was a no-brainer. We decided on the Vanagon.

"How 'bout I check out Paulson's VW during the week and get brochures and prices?" I said.

"Sounds like a plan. See if they can get a white one and probably automatic. I don't want you worrying about shifting if I need help." Bob knew exactly what he wanted, but it seemed nothing was easy anymore.

I visited Paulson's, the local VW dealer. Never having bought a car on my own before, the salesman quickly picked up on both my inexperience and the "must-have" situation. After more than thirty minutes of pleasantries, checking out the real thing, looking at brochures and listening to unnecessary explanations, I still couldn't pin him down to pricing. Not even a ballpark figure.

I patiently waited while the salesman shuttled back and forth between his desk and the manager. I began to get irritated with this little game. After all, I wasn't going to buy today, I just wanted information.

When my watch indicated an hour had passed, I said, "My husband needs to be picked up at work (which he did). I have to leave right now."

"Oh. Well, this will only take a few more minutes."

"Sorry. I don't have a few more minutes."

I walked out of the showroom.

The noon pickup was a necessary break for Bob. There were things Patricia couldn't help with. It was a little past noon when I settled Bob in the car. He could tell right away the morning expedition had not gone well.

I rehashed the events at Paulson's and concluded with, "I will *not* go back to that dealer. We have to find another dealership or forget about a VW."

Even as I said the words, a light flashed in my head, *For forty years you've taken charge, done this sort of thing; I can't do this by myself. How will I survive without you?* Abruptly I brushed the thought aside only to watch the elephant snag it.

Bob took charge. His legs were growing steadily weaker and his arms had betrayed him long ago, but his mind was as sharp as ever. He made the contacts and preliminary negotiations by phone. I made arrangements for an appointment. In a couple of days, the three of us made the thirty-minute drive to Santa Barbara, ready to complete the necessary paperwork and finalize the deal.

The white chariot stood prepped and waiting for us on the lot. It gleamed. Carolyn hauled the wheelchair out of the car, settled Bob in, and pushed him over to the van. As we walked toward it, a voice from behind said, "Mrs. Ball?"

"Yes?"

"I'm Becky. I talked with you on the phone."

"Oh, yes! Nice to meet you."

Solidly built with short dark hair, she wore no-nonsense clothes and comfortable shoes for walking around this extensive lot. She smiled and extended her hand. Her grip was strong. Then turning to Bob she greeted him warmly and offered her hand. He dreaded these awkward moments.

"He's unable to use his hands," I said matter-of-factly.

For a second her neck flushed. Then, reaching for his hand she enclosed it in her own. A gesture filled with such empathy that for a moment I couldn't speak. "Nice to meet you in person—not just a voice on the phone." She smiled at him, "Would you like to take it out for a spin?"

Bob shook his head. "Nope. We know that's the one."

We were completing the paperwork when she said, "I'll need medical confirmation of your disability."

Ooff! Anyone could sit in a wheelchair and pretend to be disabled. "I didn't think to bring it. Will it be all right if I fax it to you as soon as we get home?"

"Well, We're not supposed to write up the discount offer without proof of disability."

I was clearly dismayed. "Will a copy of the disability placard do until I can fax the medical statement to you?"

She paused for a moment, then wrinkled her nose and nodded. "That'll be all right."

"Oh, thank you. I really appreciate you doing this."

A thousand points of light. Becky was one of them. One of the many bright lights we met along the way.

When someone you love is diagnosed with Lou Gehrig's, you learn lots of facts about the disease. But those facts are only words until you confront them in a real-life situation.

I knew Bob could not drive the van.

I knew he could not even get into the van until we had a lift installed.

But when I got into the VW by myself, my eyes began to mist. This was wrong. Bob should be driving, savoring the smell and feel of a new car, enjoying the responsiveness of the machine to his touch, listening for any creaks or rattles. This virgin voyage should be his not mine.

I let out a great sigh. Such a trivial thing in light of what lay ahead. My chest began to ache. Heartache. Another nail in the coffin. As I carefully drove the white vehicle off the lot and started down 101, the tears spilled over and ran down my cheeks. I loved him so much; no wonder my heart ached.

You've got to be tough.

By the time I parked in the driveway the tears were gone, replaced by a smile.

Even before we got him out of the sedan and into the wheelchair, he asked, "How did it drive?"

"Good car. It handles well," I replied. "You will like it."

◆ ◆ ◆

We bought our first brand-new, fresh-from-the-showroom car in 1956, a forest-green Volkswagen Beetle. It was a thing of beauty.

It was a slug.

Don't get me wrong. It was great on the straightaway, and downhill it was unbeatable, but uphill? We practically had to push it. Bob would shift down and lean forward over the steering wheel, silently beseeching it to go faster. The eighteen-wheelers would come up on our rear bumper and blast the air horn until we found a place to pull over, and then flash their lights as they roared by.

When Margie was six months old we planned a cross-country trip with our new Bug–both new Bugs. We couldn't wait to share the wunderkind with the new grandparents.

As if we were the first to ever experience the astonishment of parenthood.

Bob discovered the port-a-crib/playpen fit like a glove in the back seat of the Beetle. With two legs on the floor and two secured all the way up, it rested on the back seat and, protected by plenty of padding, made a nice little nest for our wee babe.

Since it was early March, on the trip east we took the southern route to avoid any possibility of snow, but on the return trip we opted for the northern route figuring that the threat of any substantial snow was past.

We were wrong.

We left Cheyenne early in the morning. Bob glanced at the leaden sky as he packed the car. "We better get moving. That sure looks like a snow sky."

By the time we got to Laramie the first flakes began to fall.

"Do you think we ought to stop?"

"No. This thing can climb a tree."

Throughout the morning, snow showers came and went. By early afternoon it was snowing in earnest. I grabbed the map to look for the next city.

"It looks like the next place to stop would be Little America."

There was now an accumulation of four to six inches on the side of the road.

"How far is that?" he asked.

"Well, the last sign we passed said forty miles, so it should be less than that."

The road stretched straight and flat in front of us.

"We can do that easy," he replied, "but we better plan on staying the night."

We traveled in silent tension, and both of us breathed a sigh of relief when the neon lights and signs for Little

America came into view. Bob signaled and slowed to turn at the first entrance. Nothing happened.

"Uh-oh," he muttered.

"What's wrong?"

He struggled with the wheel as the car continued down the road.

"Something's wrong with the steering," Bob said, braking on and off as he tried to guide the car off the highway. At this point a large apron of asphalt extended from the road to a gas station. He managed to get the car over and stopped it parallel to the highway.

"You okay?" Bob asked, looking over at me clutching a sleeping baby.

"Fine. What's wrong with the car?"

"Haven't the foggiest. Stay here."

He bolted out the door, disappeared behind the car, and a few minutes later hustled over to the gas station. In a couple of minutes he emerged, followed by the gas station attendant. A volley of hammering sounds came from the rear of the car, then the car door opened and Bob scooted behind the steering wheel. Slipping the key into the ignition, the car started at his touch. Moving slowly, he inched forward and then turned the wheel. The car readily obeyed. He gave the service man a thumbs-up and rolled over to the pumps.

"What was the matter?"

"You won't believe it." He smiled as he climbed out to pay for the gas.

There was nothing wrong with our little Bug. The problem was snow. We had driven on a straight stretch of highway for so long that the snow thrown up by the tires had built up and filled the wheel well. The friction from the tires kept us rolling straight ahead, but when Bob tried to turn the car, the impacted layer of snow stopped us cold.

The rest of the trip was uneventful, but Bob's passion for the open road grew even deeper during that trip and lasted a lifetime.

◆ ◆ ◆

The chair slowly inched forward. Carolyn and I stood in the lobby of the medical supply house watching Connie, the overseer of the prescription wheelchair, instruct Bob in the use of the chin control. Since he was unable to use his hands, he could not operate the joystick normally used to control motorized chairs. The chin control, fastened by a flexible arm to the chair's framework, could be placed under his chin or swiveled out of the way when he needed to be pushed or became fatigued.

"Good, Mr. Ball; now try to turn to the right." Connie waved her arm to the right of the chair.

Slowly the chair turned to the right.

"Very good! You're a quick study. Now, to back it up, just use slight backward pressure. You probably won't be going in reverse very often—only if you get stuck somewhere or find yourself in tight quarters."

"I'm impressed," Bob remarked. "This responds so easily and, for such a large piece of equipment, it turns on a dime. How do we care for the battery?"

"That's going to be your job," she said as she turned toward Carolyn and me. "There are two of them and they're *very* heavy. After a day of use, they have to be recharged. Plug them in to any electrical socket—usually overnight. Actually the chair is very heavy. You have assistant controls that allow you to power the chair when you are pushing it. Like over a doorsill or repositioning it in the van." She turned to demonstrate the set of controls on the back of the chair. It was gone.

"Mr. Ball?" Her voice echoed in the empty space.

With his newfound mobility, Bob and the chair had disappeared. We hurried out of the lobby to find him.

At one time, I was assigned to a school for children with serious physical disabilities. Josh was eight. He was born with spina bifida and had never walked. One of the local service organizations generously offered to provide him with a motorized wheelchair. I was there the day it arrived and watched as Josh was gently transferred to the chair and taught how to make it move. The excitement reflected in his face was electric.

About noon, one of the staff stuck her head into the conference room where we were gathered and asked, "Has anybody seen Josh? We can't find him anywhere."

We were about to reply when she exclaimed, "Oh, no! There he goes!"

Turning to follow her gaze out the window, we caught a glimpse of the top of his head as he rounded the corner and headed out of the schoolyard. Two of the teachers raced after him and caught up with him just as he reached the street—one of the main arteries leading into the city. When he was finally corralled and safely returned to the building, the retrieving teacher commented, "I told him he mustn't ever do that again. I really couldn't get angry with him. Can you imagine how heady it must be to have freedom of movement for the first time in your life?"

Freedom. It was only a sliver, but for the first time in months Bob could move on his own. We found him in the parking lot circling the van with a broad smile on his face. I bent and kissed his cheek.

"Well, Hi-yo, Silver! How's it ride?"

"Pretty smooth. I won't win any races but, then again, I never had any desire to."

After signing the prerequisite papers, we moved back out to the parking lot. Bob drove his chair. I walked beside him. It was a nice feeling.

The lift was equipped with switches intended to be used by the disabled person, but either Carolyn or I would have to operate them. I lowered the lift to the ground and watched Bob maneuver the chair on to the platform. Carolyn set the brake, I raised the rear flap and flipped the switch. The lift rose smoothly and stopped parallel with the van floor. I hit another switch and the platform swung easily into the van.

Any concerns we had about the ability of this small lift to carry the full weight of Bob and the chair vanished. Carolyn hopped into the van, released the brake on the wheelchair, repositioned Bob, set the brake, and secured the wheelchair with the tie-downs. We would go through this routine multiple times each day. It would become automatic, like breathing.

"Can you see out the windows okay?" I glanced at him in the rearview mirror.

"Oh, yeah. I'm really glad we settled on this. It's filled with light, it looks good, and it smells great. The way a new car should."

This time as I drove off the lot, Bob shared the experience with me.

We slowed to a stop at a busy intersection. As we waited for the light to turn green, a truck rolled through the crossing carrying a load of crushed cars, layers of scrap metal. Bob watched it roll by and in a reflective mood observed, "Just think, once they were shiny new, driven off the showroom floor or the dealer's lot and parked in a driveway. Somebody's pride and joy. Now they're junk. Destined for the scrap heap. Everything in this world is transitory, from those once shiny new cars to you and me."

CHAPTER 16

*I*t was late. Carolyn was already in bed. We'd stayed up to watch the ten o'clock news, and now I was getting Bob into his pajamas. I really don't know how it happened: one minute I was pulling on his pajama bottoms, and the next minute he was on the floor. He didn't fall; he just sort of slipped out of my grasp.

"Carolyn!" I yelled.

"Are you all right?" I asked Bob, kneeling beside him.

"I seem to be, except that I'm down here on the floor."

"Honey, I'm so sorry. I must not have had a good grip on you. Now, what do we do?"

Carolyn appeared in the room, her robe half on. "Aw-oh! Well, Mr. Bob! That's a strange place to go to sleep." Then looking at me, she asked "Shall we try to get him up?"

We crawled around him trying to figure out what to do.

"I could call Carl," Carolyn suggested.

"The whole neighborhood is dark. Besides, we're going to need more than Carl," I murmured as Bob's arm fish-flopped out of my grasp.

"What about that?" Carolyn nodded towards the Hoyer lift standing in the corner. A heavy-duty piece of equipment we would eventually need, but hadn't used yet.

"I don't think this is the time to learn how to use that. Well,

Darlin," I said to Bob, "desperate situations call for desperate measures. I'm calling 9-1-1."

"Ah," he said, "a stellar idea."

They answered on the first ring. "9-1-1. What is your emergency?"

"I don't know if this is the right place to call, but I need some help. My husband has Lou Gehrig's disease, and I was in the process of transferring him from his wheelchair to the bed and he slipped out of my grasp down to the floor. I can't get him up."

"Is he injured?"

"No, no. He's fine. He just can't move on his own, and I can't lift him."

"We'll send the fire department out to assist you."

"Oh, thank you. Please tell them no sirens. The neighborhood's asleep, and this is not an emergency situation."

She repeated the information and said they were on the way.

I hung up the phone. "Well, the fire department is coming. Really nice lady. Carrie, would you run turn on the porch light?"

When Carolyn returned, we hunkered down beside Bob. "You're awfully quiet," I said.

"There's not much I can do."

"You could sing," Carolyn volunteered brightly.

"Oh, for sure, that would drive the firemen away!" Bob grinned.

Dear Carrie. Always able to lighten the moment.

The glow of flashing red lights bounced off the bedroom walls.

"Here they come. Would you go let them in?" I glanced at Carrie.

As she walked out of the room, I gently hugged Bob's shoulders. "I'm sorry you have to go through this," I murmured as I gave him a quick kiss.

"All part of the adventure."

Carolyn came back, followed by three burly firemen. They

looked about the room, which I suddenly saw through their eyes: three wheelchairs, a lift, a hospital bed. We were better equipped than some nursing homes.

"You can see our problem." I shrugged. "My husband, Bob, has ALS, Lou Gehrig's disease. Somehow I managed to drop him. His muscles are wasted. He can't move, and he can't be picked up by the arms or they may pull out of the sockets."

"You want him on the bed?"

"Please."

Without a word, they positioned themselves around Bob and slipped their arms underneath him. On signal, they lifted all 185 pounds of him as if he were a piece of Dresden china and laid him gently on the bed. Poetry in motion. It was beautiful.

"Thank you. We really appreciate it."

Carolyn escorted them to the door. As quickly and quietly as they had come, they were gone. Silent heroes. I got Bob settled for the night.

Next morning, Bob looked at me and asked, "Were there three big firemen in our bedroom last night or did I imagine it?"

"Oh, yeah, they were here. Complete with flashing red lights and a big fire truck in our driveway," I answered, looking chagrined.

We were doing range-of-motion exercises. He was the robot, I was the battery. Twice a day, every day, each muscle and joint gently stretched, bent, or rotated. Like doing jumping jacks in bed: lift the arm over the head, out to the side, across the chest, back to the side, down. Again. The muscles would never come back, but the exercises kept his extremities from contracting. His leg muscles still offered some resistance but were too weakened to provide movement or balance. I could hoist him to a standing position, and those massive tree trunks allowed him to remain upright for a few seconds if he could lean against the bed or someone was within arm's reach to keep him steady. Last night was a fluke, but a stark reminder that he was getting weaker.

"Don't you get tired of doing the same thing day after day?"

"As long as I'm doing it with you, it's not tiresome." I leaned down and kissed him.

Except for the hours when Patricia took over at work, the focus of our actions centered on Bob. From the moment he awoke until he was settled in for the night, he occupied our thoughts and activities. Think of *everything* you do in the morning to get ready for the day ahead and then think of not being able to do any of it for yourself, knowing you are totally dependent, waiting for someone else to tend to the most private of needs.

By now we had worked out a routine. First thing in the morning I'd grab the urinal and take care of that necessary chore. Then, while Bob was still in bed, range-of-motion exercises: arms, hands, fingers, legs, and feet. The exercise routine took about thirty minutes. Sometimes Carolyn would help, but usually she was getting herself ready for the day and fixing breakfast.

Exercises done, we'd generally take a break, reading from *Daily Light* and spending a few minutes in prayer. Then back to the daily ritual. Remove his pjs and raise the head of the hospital bed to put him in a sitting position. Every time I raised or lowered the bed, I mentally thanked Rita for saying, "You want one that's motorized."

With Bob now upright in bed, I'd swing his legs over the side, pull him into a standing position, and transfer him to the small wheelchair. Push the wheelchair into the bathroom and brush his teeth. Turn the shower on, check the water temperature, and then, thanks to the remodeled shower, wheel him through the shower door, and transfer him to the shower chair. A somewhat risky undertaking since we were working in water and the shower-wall we wheeled through was glass. When I thought about it, I was overwhelmed by

Bob's absolute confidence in my ability to heft him about.

As decades earlier I had soaped and rinsed wee babes from head to toe, Bob was now subjected to the same ritual. With daily ablutions out of the way, we shifted to the next phase: drying, combing, shaving, and dressing. Dressing required multiple steps of sitting him on the edge of the bed, standing him upright, sitting down again, manipulating legs into pants, arms into sleeves. Making sure all accouterments—belt, shoes, tie—were successfully secured.

At last, presentable for public viewing, Bob was transferred to his motorized chair. Once there, he savored that limited smidgen of independence as he drove himself down the hallway and into the family room, where Carolyn waited to feed him breakfast. As he hotdogged down the hall, it was my turn to shower and dress.

Time was our nemesis. The minutes just kept ticking away. There was no way to speed up the process.

Bob never complained. He never grumbled. His high-octane Type A personality accepted what God had permitted to come into his life. With this acceptance came the certain knowledge God is not blindsided by the events that occur in our lives. Bob could still trust in the God of all comfort. There was a peace that settled over him even though he knew he would never get better, only worse.

"We'd like to profile Mr. Ball in a local segment for the MDA Telethon," Rita's voice sounded over the telephone. "Follow him for a day. What do you think?"

"What do you mean?"

"Are you familiar with the MDA Telethon?"

"Yes."

"A film crew would come to your home and spend the day filming Mr. Ball, both at home and at work. You won't have to do anything special, just do whatever you do everyday. They'll work in an interview with you and Mr. Ball and one with Carolyn, too."

"How much would you want to film?" I asked. "I mean, it takes about an hour-and-a-half to get him dressed and ready for work in the morning. That's before he's even had his breakfast. We're talking about ten o'clock or later before he's ready to leave for the office."

"Oh," she interjected, "that's what we want. The things you do every day."

"Even getting him dressed?"

"Everything."

"Let me talk to Bob about it after work. Give me a number where I can reach you in the morning."

Of course, Bob agreed. MDA had appeared as a beacon in this shadowy journey. All the doctors we encountered prior to diagnosis knew about the disease, but it was a textbook knowledge. If they had seen a patient with ALS, it was usually in the early stages of the disease before a diagnosis had been made. MDA didn't just know ALS, they became ALS. They helped us understand it and live with it. If Bob's participation in the telethon would help raise funds to find the cause or discover a cure for this unrelenting disease with its ravenous appetite, it was the least he could do.

On a sunny morning in April, the crew arrived accompanied by Rita. We had half-finished the morning ritual, but had stopped short of shaving, putting on Bob's shoes, and breakfast. The crew went to work. They filmed everything. Five hours out of our day captured on film. The whole thing eventually condensed to approximately eight-minutes for the telethon.

At noon, Jann Carl arrived; she would act as emcee for the local MDA outreach. Vivacious, lovely, perpetually cheerful, never at a loss for words, she would conduct the interview. Not an easy task. A balancing act between sensitivity and pity, staying away from intrusive questions while trying to capture an intimate moment that would cause viewers to reach for their checkbooks. She succeeded.

She asked Bob, "What's the most difficult to handle?"

He paused, his blue eyes blurred with tears, and there was a catch in his voice when he replied, "Not being around to watch my grandchildren grow up."

It was a poignant moment.

◆　◆　◆

It was love at first sight.

Protective, possessive love.

Bob adored his little Margie. "How is it you can love a stranger?" he mused, as he cuddled her gently in his arms. "She comes into our lives, brings nothing with her, and demands everything from us. The funny thing is, I'm not only eager to provide for her, I can't imagine life without her! She surely has me wrapped around her perfect little finger."

Every night after dinner he would prop her on his lap and discuss the events of the day. Her day.

"And how was your day today?"

He would listen with undivided attention as she cooed. When she paused, he would interject, "And what else?" or "Uh-huh, I thought so," or "You don't say." As she grew, she became expert in babbling, often carrying on her part of the conversation nonstop for five or six minutes.

Sometimes he sang, often crooning a tender lullaby while walking back and forth with Margie on his shoulder.

It was a tranquil interval. The three of us in our little nest. Like first-time parents everywhere, we were awed by each new accomplishment, no matter how small, and shared the sense of wonder she found in the things that had become commonplace: butterflies and snowflakes, flowers and kittens.

With each child, Bob's love grew and so did his responsibility, not only to provide for their physical needs but to fill his role as daddy.

But the years passed, and the children grew too old for bedtime stories and lullabies.

And then, a serendipity.

"Du, du, du bist..."

The sound came from the bedroom.

Quietly I walked down the hall and peeked through the partially open bedroom door. Bob hung over the crib patting Stevie's back. The melody of the old lullaby circled softly in the air. Silently, I turned and walked back towards the kitchen. I couldn't keep the smile off my face. When David was an infant, if Daddy stopped singing he would lift his head from Bob's shoulder and say, "Du," meaning sing it again. This singular melody had comforted all three children.

Now, here was Bob crooning the same refrain to his grandson.

◆ ◆ ◆

A second. A blink. A moment ago I held my little ones in my arms. Now they cuddled wee ones of their own. I had heard it all my life: "Where has the time gone?" Now I could relate. I suddenly felt the passage of time like a raging river recklessly sweeping under my feet and threatening to knock me off balance. Great chunks of life passed us by in a twinkling. Gone. And what of those chunks? Were they lost forever? No. Forever stored in memory banks, which were in turn triggered by the pictures Bob had faithfully taken over the years.

Both the Muscular Dystrophy Association, MDA, and the ALS Association, ALSA, were indispensable. We were profoundly grateful for both organizations. The handbooks provided by ALSA contained valuable insights into the progression of the disease and useful information on necessary equipment, plus a wealth of tips and advice for both caregiver and patient. The MDA offered assistance in the ALS clinics and multiple workshops for living with ALS.

One Thursday evening we arrived at an MDA-ALS workshop to find we were the only ones in attendance: one patient to two instructors. After waiting to see if anyone else would show up, the nurse went into her instructional spiel about nutrition, proper chewing, and swallowing.

Finishing up she said, "Since you're the only ones here, do you have any specific questions about eating or about anything else for that matter."

"Oh, yes." I hesitated, "It's getting harder and harder to turn Bob over at night. Maybe I'm not going about it the right way. Could you show us how to do that?"

"Oh, that can be difficult. Tell me about your sleeping arrangements."

"Well, let's see. Right now we have a king headboard with a twin bed attached on one side and a hospital bed for Bob on the other side." I gestured with my hands. "His bed snuggles up next to mine. In fact, when the whole thing is made up with king-sized top sheet and covers, you really can't tell there's a hospital bed there."

"You don't get out of bed then to turn him?" she asked.

"No. Although the two beds do swing apart, at night, when we're sleeping, I try to make as little disturbance as possible so we can get back to sleep. Just get up on my knees, slide my hands under him, and pull him towards me."

"Have you tried a draw-sheet? A short length of sheet placed under him that you pull to turn him?"

"Without much success. In fact, it doesn't work at all. I suppose if I were to stand beside the bed it might work, but on my knees…," my voice trailed off.

"Putting your hands under his torso and sliding him, like this, should work," she demonstrated putting her hands straight out in front of her and then cupping them upward as if she were carrying wood for the fire. "You want to pull him towards you until he is on his back, slide your hands under his back, grasp his other side and tip him up. It's almost one motion. You may need to do a little repositioning."

"Maybe I'm not using the right leverage. If we put Bob on that bed," I pointed toward the hospital bed in the room, "could you show me how?"

"Good idea. In fact, let's push the other bed up next to it, and I'll get on it on my knees and turn him." She already was moving towards the second bed, and quickly maneuvered it into place and set the brake. Meanwhile Carolyn and I transferred Bob from wheelchair to bed and got him settled into a sleeping position facing the empty bed.

"You okay?" I asked him. He nodded. "Do you mind if we do this?" *A little late for me to be asking him that*, I thought.

"Of course not. Anything that will make it easier."

"All right. Is this typical?" the nurse asked.

"Well, he's usually not fully clothed." I grinned. "But he does start on his left side."

She knelt on the second bed. "What you want to do is slide him toward you so there's enough room in his bed to turn him over." She slid her hands under his torso and…nothing.

Learning how to care for a comatose or nonresponsive patient requires hands-on practice. When you practice on someone, usually a willing participant, they automatically help a little. Even if you tell them to play dead, the muscles involuntarily come into play. Putting these same techniques into practice in real-life situations may not work so easily.

Bob couldn't move *at all*. He was a big man. Dead weight.

Not like moving a tree trunk, more like trying to lift a giant, floppy fish with your bare hands.

"Hmmmm." She repositioned her arms and tried again. Nothing. "Well, hmmmm. Okay. Let's try this again." Then, with much tugging and a face red from exertion, she got him over. Leaning back on her haunches, she looked at me and said, "You're not a very hefty person, and it's harder to do when you're on your knees. I guess you're going to need help."

Sitting on the floor, his trunk resting on the bed, the elephant watched.

CHAPTER 17

"Carolyn, I've got a problem."

She looked at me with raised eyebrows.

"Remember the other night at the workshop when we talked about turning Dad?"

"Mmmm." She nodded.

"In addition to it being hard to turn him, the time between position changes is getting shorter. I've been turning him four or five times a night. Problem is, I'm exhausted. Not getting a solid night of sleep in weeks. Would you be willing to switch beds for one night so I can get some uninterrupted sleep?"

"Oh, sure. I'm stronger than you anyway. I can probably turn him easier. Have you talked to Dad about this? Is it okay?"

"Not yet. But I'm not going to make a habit of it—maybe twice a month?"

"Hey, that's great, but make sure it's okay with Mr. Bob. He's kind of possessive about his caregiver, you know." She smiled, but I knew she was serious.

I didn't ask permission; just told him I needed sleep and Carolyn would spell me. Worked out fine.

Two weeks later we did it again.

"Mom! Mom! Wake up!"

Reluctantly I opened my eyes. Carolyn's stricken face hovered above the bed. Instantly I was wide awake. "What's the matter?" I asked as I threw the covers back and struggled to sit up.

"I, we were just going to let you get a little extra sleep, and I tried to get him up by myself. I'm so sorry."

"Is he okay?" I questioned, heading towards the bedroom.

"Not really. He hit his head on the dresser on the way down." She was a light shade of gray.

Bob was stretched out on the floor. A scene that looked eerily familiar. I knelt down and bent over him. "Ouch. Hey, Hon, does your head hurt?"

"Now, don't get upset with Carolyn," he looked at me with those swimming-pool-blue eyes. "I told her it was okay."

"I don't see a pool of blood. Let's have a look at the back of your head." Gently I tried to lift his head. I couldn't move it. "Guess we'll have to wait to get a good look at you until we get you up." I turned to Carolyn, "It's not the first time he's landed on the floor, and it probably won't be the last. So buck up, stiff upper lip, and all that stuff. I need your help. This appears to be as good a time as any to learn to use that lift in the corner."

That morning it took longer than it ever would again, but when we finally got the rig assembled and the sling positioned under Bob, Carolyn turned the crank and slowly he lifted into space. We let out a cheer. Bob rewarded us with the ghost of a grin. It was a bittersweet victory. We knew it meant we had entered another phase. And, yes, he did need stitches.

The program Bob had purchased for his computer worked flawlessly. It scanned the keyboard at a steady pace, which he could adjust to his own skill level. When the letter he wanted lit up, he was supposed to press a switch or lever, and it would show up on the monitor. Since the muscles in his hands and fingers had atrophied, the leg muscle controlling his right knee was the only viable option.

He used the outside of his knee to press a feather-light switch attached to the frame of his wheelchair, and the text appeared letter-by-letter on the monitor.

It was a lengthy and fatiguing process, but it worked. From time to time he used the augmentative communication device, becoming familiar with the program and listening to the different voices as they "spoke" the words he printed on the screen. Every so often a little girl voice would narrate what was printed, causing me to startle and Carolyn to comment, "Why, Mr. Bob, what an angelic voice you have."

To which he'd reply, "My alter ego."

So far, it was more of an electronic gadget to demonstrate for visitors than a medical necessity. But we knew what it meant, someday his own voice would be silent. I was still in denial about that stage of ALS and shoved the thought aside whenever it crept in. I could not imagine Bob without his voice.

◆　◆　◆

Bob's voice.

He loved being a DJ. During those early radio days at the CBS station in Klamath Falls, he was responsible for several hours of music each day. Sitting at the console he felt totally in control, thoroughly competent. Speaking into the microphone to an unseen audience came naturally to him. He knew exactly what to do, how to blend the music, cue the records, what to say, how much to say. He was never at a loss for words. Totally at ease.

On Saturdays, he hosted a Country Gospel Music program. The music, performed mainly by quartets and the occasional soloist, got your toes to tappin'. One Saturday evening he came home and said, "You know, I really like Country Gospel music."

I looked at him doubtfully. This was the man who loved opera and all things classical. The man whose eyes filled with tears when he sang the last line of Wesley's stirring hymn: "Amazing love! How can it be that Thou my God shouldst die for me?"

"Forever why?" I asked.

"When you really listen to the words, they're almost always about heaven, and there's such a joyful longing, such an eagerness to be there. Seems as if we've forgotten where we're headed," he continued. "We've lost our focus."

I began to listen, really listen to the words. He was right, of course. Songs like "I'll Fly Away," "First Day in Heaven," "Just Over in the Gloryland," "Hallelujah We Shall Rise," "The Old Gospel Ship," "We'll Understand it Better By and By," "Life's Railway to Heaven," and "Will the Circle be Unbroken?" all expressed yearning for our eternal destination.

Bob never lost his focus on eternity. With sure steps, he knew where he was headed. And the path of the DJ? Well, that was a different story. The practical side of his nature took over. DJs made about as much as dishwashers. So, as much as Bob loved it, when family came along, he ventured into radio advertising sales and then into management. But that first love of sitting at the console and speaking into the microphone never went away, it just got buried under tons and tons of living.

His voice.

Before I grew to love his soul and innermost being, I fell in love with his voice. His bass voice resonated over the phone lines. I suppose he was as intrigued by the sound of this newly acquired deep voice as I was. As he matured, the voice mellowed and settled. And then, a captive audience—children.

Beginning with Margie, bedtime was steeped in ritual:

bath, story, prayer, and a kiss. Night after night the same routine. A story at bedtime always had a calming effect. By the time the children reached two, four, and six, books were sought-after treasures. There were old standbys they asked for again and again. They knew them by heart, but listened contentedly to the cadence of familiar words, eagerly anticipating the events on the next page. When a new book was introduced, it often became "the favorite" for a week or so and then gradually found its place among the treasury of children's books. Most of their books looked like the velveteen rabbit: falling apart from love and use.

I was usually the designated reader, but when Bob read with his deep base voice, the children were mesmerized. The cast of characters filled the room and marched around in living color. Timothy Tiger appeared to be on the verge of growling, Horton sounded incredibly weary, the Grinch more wicked, and Bunny and Duckling utterly adorable. The resonance of his voice gave the characters new life, yet the words were still familiar, still comfortable. Perhaps that's why it was so special when Daddy read.

And then, after a lengthy interlude, *redux*. The very same stories we read to the children when they were small were now read to the grandchildren. Stevie, protectively snuggled in Grandpa's lap, listened with rapt attention. When the last page was read and the book closed, he would pat the cover and say, "'gain."

Then came Tim.

Then Catherine.

Then ALS.

◆　◆　◆

By the end of summer the aggressive disease began to affect Bob's speech. It was subtle—a slight slurring. Consonants, once crisp and precise, were now soft and indistinct. People asked him to repeat. We tried to ignore it, but Bob could hear it. This cruel disease, not content with taking away the use of his limbs, now began to destroy his speech muscles. Dependent on his voice for his livelihood, this was the *coup de grace*.

To compensate, he talked slower, exaggerating the enunciation of troublesome words, substituting softer consonant sounds wherever possible. For the most part, face-to-face conversation was easily understood. If the word was still questionable, the context made it clear. But telephone negotiations were becoming more difficult. The ease with which he had handled decades of business deals, smoothed ruffled feathers, or calmed disgruntled producers was now replaced with increasing anxiety as he tried to make himself understood.

An associate was hired to learn from Bob and eventually take over the necessary telephone contacts. Bob was supportive and gracious, but how do you teach in a few months what took decades to acquire? Sort of like teaching your child to drive. You've done it for so long, you just know when to start turning the steering wheel or depressing the brake pedal. Only with practice will the teen gain a feel for it. Bob did not have the luxury of time.

In mid-September the bottom fell out. An account he had nurtured for more than twenty years elected to move to another broadcast outlet, a competitor. His coworker, inexperienced at negotiations, let it slip away. Bob was still at home that morning when the news came. I turned on the speaker phone and stood by in case he needed help. Although the brief conversation with his colleague was civil, the look in his eyes spoke volumes.

Frustration.

Despair.

Defeat.

Using his chin control, he whipped his chair around in ever tighter circles. Pausing in this frenetic activity he stared at me. "T'is shou' nefer haf haben. Wha' am I gonna' do?"

The words betrayed the depth of his grief. I wanted to throw my arms around him and tell him it didn't matter, but an elephant sat in his lap, and I couldn't get close enough.

In his characteristic approach to all things pertaining to life and living, Bob put the incident under the microscope, acknowledged his loss of influence, and moved on. It was not an act of ultimate resignation, but one of peaceful acceptance. It was the knowledge that God was in control and the events that invaded his life were not random happenings but rather a plan set in motion by the Creator for our growth and His glory.

Now we faced a new hurdle. The same muscles that controlled Bob's speaking ability operated his swallowing mechanism. Carolyn made lots of things that would go down easy, soft foods like mashed potatoes, chili, Jell-O, pudding, and meatloaf.

Contrary to what we thought, liquids were very difficult for him to get down. I assumed that liquids would be fine, but, when the swallowing mechanism is compromised, the liquids come at you too fast and you can't control them. On our next visit to the clinic, the doctor confirmed that although a liquid diet is generally considered to be the easiest to digest, it is not suitable for the ALS patient since it may induce choking or aspiration, the very thing you want to avoid.

"Swallow for me."

With his hand gently swaddling Bob's neck, the doctor felt the movement. "Is mealtime becoming more difficult?"

Bob looked at me. "We're extremely careful," I volunteered, "but there's not an awful lot he can swallow. And he's really apprehensive, with good cause, about aspirating anything into his lungs."

"I think it's time you considered a feeding tube. We can connect you up with a permanent drip or semi-permanent at set times during the day."

We looked at each other warily. Bob had no interest in being attached to a permanent IV drip. Observing the look we exchanged, the doctor added, "Barbara can hand do it at regular meal times." He looked at me, "The caveat is you need to introduce the food very slowly because it will go directly into his stomach."

"When you say food, what do you mean?" I asked.

"Something already prepared and chock-full of nutrients, like Ensure."

"If I feed him he won't need to be tethered to anything, is that right?"

"Right. And with a feeding tube in place he won't have to worry about choking, and it will give him at least another three months."

Everything in the office went gray. The doctor's last words hung there like a neon sign blinking on and off: THREE MONTHS, THREE MONTHS, THREE MONTHS. It was another out-of-body occurrence. I shouldn't have been shocked by the prediction. When Bob was diagnosed, the doctor told us most patients with ALS live about three years from the onset. Three months from now would bring us up on three years. Since that initial prognosis, however, no one had so much as hinted at a timeline. You get lulled into thinking things will just continue on and on.

I pulled back from the fog to hear the doctor saying, "Let them know what day is best for you."

"Hon?" It was Bob's voice. I suddenly realized both the doctor and Bob were staring at me, waiting for some response.

"I'm sorry. What were you saying?"

"Gretchen will arrange a time for the procedure. Stop by the desk on your way out and give her a couple of dates that will work for you."

It was already dusk when we headed towards home. With Bob secured in the back and Carolyn sitting next to him in case he needed anything, I sat in the front alone. As the VW cut through the gathering darkness, the tears slid unbidden down my checks when the rhythmic whir of the tires on the highway seemed to repeat the doctor's words: three months, three months, three months. *I want more.*

We were early. We parked in a handicapped spot and sat in the hospital parking lot. This was considered an outpatient procedure, even though we would check into the hospital and be assigned a room, something about meeting the insurance restrictions if the stay would be less than twenty-three hours. The clock started ticking once we checked in. After being assigned a room and outfitted in appropriate hospital attire, a nasogastric tube would be inserted and Bob would be wheeled to surgery to have the feeding tube surgically implanted through the abdominal wall. Placement would be verified through radiography (x-ray). Then he would be returned to his room. If he remained stable for six hours after the procedure, the nasogastric tube would be removed and feeding through the abdominal tube could be initiated to make sure everything worked okay. All within the twenty-three-hour time frame.

By this time Carolyn had parked her car and climbed into the van.

"There's no point in all of us being here," I told her. "If you just hang around long enough to help me get Dad into the hospital and wait while we get checked in, you might as well head for the mall or rent a video or soak in the tub. I won't let him out of my sight while we're here, and I'll drive us home in the morning."

"Are you sure you don't want me to stay with you?"

"There are plenty of nurses around here to assist and, besides, you deserve a little break."

"What about in the morning? Do you want me to come and get you?"

"I don't think so. I'll give you a call if I need extra help."

With preliminaries done and the nasogastric tube in place, Bob's gurney was parked outside the small surgical room. We waited for him to be admitted.

"Mr. Ball?" The young nurse headed towards the gurney. She smiled sweetly at us. "Are you Mr. Ball?"

"He is," I responded.

She began to push the gurney towards the door. I walked alongside.

"I'm sorry," she said to me, "you'll have to wait out here."

"Where he goes, I go. Mr. Ball has Lou Gehrig's disease. I'm his hands and voice."

"Oh. Just a minute." She disappeared into the room and then reappeared a few minutes later. "Okay. You can come in."

They readied Bob for the procedure. I hovered near his head, as far away from the abdominal wall as I could get.

"You doing okay?" I asked and was answered with a reassuring blink.

From time to time I kissed his cheek, or forehead, or nose, and repeatedly asked him how he was getting along.

After what seemed like hours but was in reality only about thirty minutes, the doctor said, "All right. We need to get a picture of this to check on the placement so you will have to step out of the room. Just follow Eileen."

I glanced at Bob. "Okay?"

Before he could even blink the doctor added, "You'll just be behind that glass over there. You can watch what's going on."

I patted Bob's cheek. "I'll be right back." He blinked.

I followed Eileen into the windowed room. As they scurried about setting up the equipment, Eileen, who apparently had been appointed my babysitter and told to keep me out of the way, began to make conversation.

"How long have you been married?"

"Going on thirty-seven years," I replied, watching Bob.

"No. I mean, how long have you been married to *this* man?"

I looked at her, trying to mask my astonishment at her question. "Thirty-seven years."

"Thirty-seven years? To the same man? You've been married thirty-seven years to each other?"

"We have." I smiled at her.

"But you act like you're so much in love," she protested.

"That's no act; we are in love."

"But after thirty-seven…"

At that moment the doctor waved us back in, and I followed Eileen through the door. As we walked into the room, she burst out with, "Guess what? They've been married thirty-seven years. Thirty-seven years to each other. Isn't that amazing? Thirty-seven years. And they're still in love."

The rest of the surgical team cast a few patronizing looks in her direction and managed a few grunts as she rattled on.

Bob was soon dispatched and we were escorted back to the room. I walked beside the gurney and waited while he was transferred into bed. Finally alone, I leaned down and nibbled on his ear.

"Imagine, thirty-seven years. Where did they go?" I murmured.

As I straightened up, to my surprise I glimpsed an elephant hunched in the corner of the room. *Now, what do you suppose he's doing here?* I wondered and then pushed the thought out of my mind.

CHAPTER 18

*H*ospital personnel flowed in and out of the room, checking Bob's blood pressure, taking his temperature, viewing the site of the feeding tube—all making sure his progress was satisfactory. At length, a tray arrived with his dinner since it would be eight o'clock or later before we could try out the feeding tube. We looked at the contents with surprise. The tag on the tray said: "Diet—liquid." And indeed it was. Bouillon and tea.

"Well, there's no way you're going to get that down. A little sip, maybe? Want to try?" I asked.

"Uh-uh," he grunted.

About an hour later someone popped in to pick up the tray. Upon viewing the untouched contents, she remarked, "Not hungry, huh? Want me to take the tray?"

"I don't know who ordered a liquid diet, but he can't manage liquids. He can swallow soft foods, like Jell-O, but that's about it."

"Want me to try and find something for you?" she asked.

I looked at Bob. He was dozing. "Thanks. But we're going to try out a feeding tube in about an hour so I think we'll just wait."

Right on schedule, the nurse arrived to remove the nasogastric tube, which had been inserted through his nostril, down his throat, and into his stomach.

"How you doing?" she asked with a cheerful smile. "I'm going to check your vitals before I take out this tube."

She stood on the right side of the bed and I moved around to the left. Carefully she removed the tape that secured the tube and, with a firm grasp and one gentle but firm tug, pulled it out. As it swished out of his nostril, it was accompanied by a great rush of vomitus.

"Quick! Lean him forward so he doesn't aspirate any of that into his lungs!"

Even as the words tumbled out of my mouth, we both placed hands on his shoulders and quickly leaned him forward.

As I helped her clean him up she commented, "Thanks. It's nice to run into somebody who knows what to do."

Now, clothed in a clean hospital gown, Bob watched while the nurse set up the IV type drip for the feeding tube. It was almost midnight.

"This will flow for the rest of the night. You can just go to sleep."

Easier said than done. Sleeping in a hospital is not for the faint of heart. Besides the usual bustle of activity, I was ensconced in a sort of lounge chair that had seen better days. Not very conducive to sleeping. Ah, well, only for a night.

I gave Bob a kiss on the cheek. "Try to get some sleep. The worst is over."

Bob's grunts got me out of the chair. It was a little past 2:00 a.m. I moved beside his bed. "What's the matter, Honey?"

"Sic." Indeed, he did not look well.

I looked at the IV bag. It was about half empty.

"Are you full?" I asked. He blinked

"Feeling nauseous?" He blinked.

"Bloated?" Before blinking he flared his eyes, which I took to mean, "Oh, yeah."

I rang for the nurse.

"Everything okay here?" she asked.

"I think maybe Bob has had enough. He's beginning to feel sick."

She checked his vitals. "Everything seems to be fine. Are you feeling nauseated?"

Bob blinked.

"And bloated," I added.

"Let me check with the floor supervisor. I'll be right back." She hurried out.

In a few minutes she returned followed by a young man. "This is Richard, my supervisor."

Holding a clipboard in front of him, Richard waved it to the side as he spoke to me. "The instructions are to administer tube feeding."

"The purpose was to ascertain that everything was working okay," I responded. "It is and he's obviously had enough. He'd like to have it disconnected."

Richard stood his ground. "I'm sorry. We can't do that."

"Of course, you can," I retorted. "Bob even looks sick. This is not a medicinal drip nor is it replacing fluids. Call the doctor for permission if you have to."

"It's almost 2:30 in the morning. I'm not going to call the doctor at this hour for something as trivial as that."

I tried to reply civilly. "Bob's well-being is not trivial."

"Sh! You're upsetting the patient."

"I am not upsetting the patient! He's already upset. He's had enough. Please disconnect the IV drip."

"Lower your voice. You're disturbing the other patients on the floor."

By now, there were three nurses in the room and one hovered outside the door. I stood between Bob and the small cohort of nurses. I was beginning to feel like a lioness protecting her cub. In a moment I might even start snarling. Maybe I already had.

Looking directly at Richard, I spoke in a level controlled voice, "If you don't have the authority to disconnect this IV drip from the feeding tube, then find someone who does. Now."

Richard stared at me for a few more seconds, then, with a sharp intake of air, turned on his heels and stalked out of the room. I wouldn't see him again, but in less than ten minutes the nurse came back into the room and disconnected the IV from the feeding tube.

"Thank you. Sorry to make such a fuss," I said. "I hope you didn't get in any trouble."

"Oh, no. Sometimes we forget that the patient is a real person." She smiled at Bob.

After she left I hovered near Bob for a few minutes.

I interpreted when he mumbled, "I hate hospitals."

"I know. Only a few more hours and we can go home. Think you can get a little sleep?"

He blinked three or four times. There was something on his mind. I listened and filled in the missing sounds as he talked. "No hospital. Am I asking too much? Will it be too hard on you to have me die at home?"

Although we both knew the outcome of ALS, this was the first time Bob had actually said the "D" word. He often spoke of death and dying, but it was generic; this was personal. I put my hands on his shoulders and laid my face next to his.

"Every minute I get to spend with you is precious. I meant it when I said in sickness and in health, till death do us part." I kissed him gently and hugged him as best I could.

"Goodnight, Love."

As I climbed into the worn lounge chair, my mind exploded with memories of another death at home; memories I'd deliberately kept buried for years.

◆ ◆ ◆

Sixteen.

The year I turned sixteen brought me face to face with the realities of life. I grew up fast that year. It was a year marked by the highest of highs, when Bob kissed me on the back steps one sultry summer evening, to the lowest of lows, when Mom died on a cold, gray day in December.

We lived in a big, old house in northern New Jersey. We'd moved into the house the summer I was fifteen. Mom marshaled a group of handymen to do her bidding. I don't know where she found them, but whenever we moved there would always be a steady stream of painters, paper hangers, plumbers, and gardeners to "get the place fixed up."

This move was no exception. For the first eight to ten weeks, the house was scrubbed, polished, waxed, and painted. It seemed there was always somebody on a ladder. Finally, in August, they were gone. Mom's touch was everywhere. You could almost feel her breathe a sigh of contentment when it was done. I suppose it made her feel settled, secure. The house now was truly hers.

The freshly painted foyer was big enough to be a room in its own right. In fact, it held my grand piano, and every time I sat down to practice I felt as if I were performing on-stage. The foyer provided access to the rest of the house. To the right, a large archway opened to the living and dining rooms. At the rear of the foyer, switchback banistered stairs led to the second floor. At the foot of the stairs was a door that led to the kitchen and basement. It was usually left open.

Whoever built the house went a little overboard with doors. When you walked through the doorway from the foyer to the kitchen, a few steps to your left was the door that went to the basement, and straight ahead another door-way, and door, that led to the kitchen. When Mom did not want to hear me practicing, she would shut the door to the foyer and the door to the kitchen. It acted like a vapor lock and kept the sound out.

After a year and a half, things had evolved into a comfortable routine. My sister was off to college. Dad was first up and out each day—walking the half mile to catch the commuter train that would take him to the business district of lower Manhattan. Mom would make sure I got out the door in enough time to walk the mile to school.

In typical adolescent self-absorption I had no idea what she did all day. The house always looked like a full page display ad for *Better Homes and Gardens*, so I knew she cleaned. The clothes in my closet were always fresh so I knew she washed and ironed. The meals we ate were always delicious, and about once a week Mom invited another family to share dinner with us. We attended church regularly, and our social life revolved around the church and its families.

In the fall of my sixteenth year, there was a subtle change. Dad bought a new car, an automatic. After so many years of stick shifts, Mom couldn't get the hang of it. She hardly ever went out. We stopped having guests over, and there was unmistakable tension between Mom and Dad. I don't know what they argued about, but I could hear their angry voices. If I walked into the room, Mom's eyes would be glaring and Dad's jaw clenched.

Once, when I walked in the kitchen, she was holding a knife at shoulder level, and I thought I heard my dad mutter, "Go ahead." Before I could react to the situation, she turned to the sink, dropped the knife into the sudsy water, and began to wash the dishes. Dad walked out the back door without a word. I wasn't quite sure what I had witnessed.

"Is everything okay?"

"Yes, dear. See if you can help Daddy with the yard."

On a cold gray morning in December, Mom and I sat at the table eating breakfast before I headed off for school. Suddenly she began to cry, not really crying, gentle weeping. "What's wrong with us? What's happening to us?"

I stared at her in confusion. Mothers are supposed to have the answers to life's problems. They're not supposed to ask questions like that of teen-aged daughters.

"Well, maybe if you and Daddy didn't fight so much..." My voice trailed off.

She sighed heavily, "You better go; you'll be late for school."

"Do you want me to stay home with you?"

"No, dear, you go."

I put on my heavy jacket and again said, "Are you sure you don't want me to stay with you?"

She shook her head.

"See ya' tonight," I said as I kissed her cheek.

I didn't want to leave her in such a state, but I walked out the door. I didn't know she was peering into the black hole of depression. I didn't know how easy it was to slip into or how hard it was to crawl out.

It was after four by the time I got home. I could tell the days were getting shorter. The last of the sun hung low in the sky, and it already looked like early evening. I grabbed the handle on the screen door. It did not open. *Must be latched*, I thought. I walked down the porch steps and headed for the back door. That screen door did not budge; it too was latched. I rang the doorbell. No response. I walked around to the front again and rang that doorbell. After waiting a bit, I pounded on the door. How could both screen doors be hooked? Maybe the hook fell when the door was slammed.

Leaving my books on the front porch, I walked around back to the detached garage. Maybe Mom had gone out. The garage was locked. I peered through the window. Nope, there was the car. I went back to the front porch and rang the bell several times. Where could she be? It wasn't like Mom to be gone when I got home. Maybe she was next door.

There was little light left outside. In desperation, I went next door to the Nelsons'. Their house was lit up and shone like a beacon in the late afternoon. I rang the bell. Their door opened almost immediately.

"Hi, Mr. Nelson. Is my mom here?"

"No," he replied, shaking his head.

"I think something is wrong. All the doors are locked, and I can't get in."

"Mabel? I'm going with Barbara. She's got a problem getting into the house." Hal Nelson grabbed his coat and walked with me to the house.

"Mom's always home. I can't imagine where she is."

"Do you have a key?"

"Yes, but all the screen doors are latched. The hook must have fallen when the door was shut. You know?"

Mr. Nelson did not respond. We tried all the doors. Then he tried the windows that overlooked the front porch. They refused to budge.

"There's still a little light," he said. "Let's try the basement windows." The third small casement window on the side of the house budged a little. He pushed hard. Suddenly the window swung inward. "Do you think you can get through there?" he asked.

I visualized Dad's workbench under the window. "Oh, yeah, I can do that."

"You wiggle through there, and I'll wait at the front door for you."

Fearful of spiders and other creeping things, I carefully worked my way through the small window while Mr. Nelson tried to hold it open. My feet touched the workbench.

"Okay. I'm on the workbench. I can make it now."

I slithered my torso through the window.

"You okay?" he questioned.

The smell of gas assaulted me. "I'm fine."

The small window banged shut.

The basement reeked of gas fumes. I could hear the furnace running. Thoughts raced through my head. *Yuck! What in the world? There must be a gas leak.* In the fading light, I quickly clambered down from the workbench, made my way to the stairs and took them two at a time. I pulled open the door at the top of the stairs, and it slammed shut behind me.

In an instant blackness engulfed me. I had never been in such utter darkness. It was smothering. It was alive. I could touch it. For a second, I stood there bewildered trying to get my bearings. *What?* The smell of gas was overwhelming. All the doors were shut: the door leading from the foyer, the door to the kitchen, and, behind me, the door to the basement. It was a small, pitch-black closet, and I was standing in it.

In that instant I knew.

"No, no, no!" Unbidden, the words spilled from my lips in a flood of anguish. I groped through the thick blackness until I felt the doorknob. Flinging open the door to the foyer, I bolted towards the front door. I wrenched it open and, as I unlatched the screen door, yelled to Mr. Nelson, "Hurry! Hurry! It's Mom!"

He raced behind me into the kitchen.

The oven door was wide open spewing forth the deadly

fumes. Mom was on the floor. A small trickle of white foam oozed from the corner of her mouth. I knelt beside her. "Oh, Mama, Mama," I groaned.

"Rub her hands!" he ordered. He flew about the kitchen turning the knobs that controlled the gas, opening doors and windows.

"Where's the phone?" he barked.

"On the stair landing."

I heard him call the ambulance. I kept talking to her as I tried to rub her hands. They flopped out of my grasp like dead fish. "Oh, Mama," I moaned, "how could you do this!"

And then the ambulance was there, and the police. Somebody took me over to the Nelsons'. I sat in a straight backed chair in their hall. They scurried about casting furtive, sympathetic glances towards me. What do you say to a sixteen-year-old whose mother has just committed suicide? *How was your day, dear?*

The clock chimed. *Daddy!*

"Mrs. Nelson? My daddy's train gets in in ten minutes. I, I think I better meet him before he comes home. Could somebody take me down to the station?"

There was a flurry of activity, and then we were in the car heading for the train station. The train had already pulled in, and a crowd of men, all looking alike in dark overcoats, paraded up the dimly lit street.

"Do you see him anywhere?" asked Mrs. Nelson.

I scanned the passengers. "There! There he is."

The car slowed and I jumped out and ran to catch up with him. I grabbed his coat. He turned.

"Why, Bobbie! What are you doing here?"

I suddenly felt very small and frightened. "It...it's Mom."

"What?" he asked as he leaned towards me. "I can't hear you, dear."

How could I tell him? I started to shiver, "It's Mom. She's dead." Of all the ways I'd thought of breaking the news to him, it certainly wasn't like that.

The Nelsons drove us home.

In the days and weeks that followed, I never cried. I was a bystander watching the events unfold. An observer, detached and insulated from the emotions that swirled around me. It was only after I held my firstborn, our Margaret Jean, in my arms and experienced the wonder of motherhood that I wept for the mother I lost, the grandmother little Margie would never know. Such a loss. Such a waste.

◆ ◆ ◆

Sleep was far from me as the memories ricocheted around in my consciousness. For decades I had blocked these recollections or shoved them deep inside because I wasn't able to confront the emotional pain they brought with them. Too much sorrow. Now I took them out and looked at them, knowing it was part of what made me strong enough to walk with Bob, even though it meant walking with him through the shadow of death.

Something was wrong. Every time I fed Bob through the tube he felt nauseated and bloated. It was not supposed to be like that. The visiting nurse stopped by and reassured us it was okay. He just needed time to adjust. By the fourth day I put in a call to our regular doctor. He was on vacation. I called the ALS clinic.

"That doesn't sound right. You better bring him in."

"Having trouble with the feeding tube?" the doctor asked as he examined the site and gently probed Bob's abdomen.

"No, the tube works fine," I replied. "But whenever I feed him, he feels sick to his stomach. As a matter of fact, it happened the first night while we were still in the hospital. He felt really awful after only half of the IV bag was emptied."

"Let's take a look."

After viewing things through the fluoroscope, the doctor met us in the exam room.

"Well, there's a problem," he began. "The tube is supposed to empty into the stomach. It should be short enough to terminate in the stomach. The one in place now is too long. It has passed through the stomach into the duodenum. Bob's food, instead of dumping into his stomach, is going directly into the duodenum. That's why he feels so bloated and nauseous every time you feed him."

"Do you mean we have to go through this again?" I grimaced as I asked the question.

"No, no. The tube can just be shortened. It won't take much time at all. Just in and out. But we'll have to make an appointment, and that may take two weeks or more. You'll probably have to go back to carefully feeding him soft foods by mouth."

"That first night in the hospital, when they were testing the feeding tube, was the food going directly into the duodenum? Is that why he felt so sick?"

"Oh, most assuredly!"

Another adventure. One we didn't need. Now I knew why that smirking elephant found his way into the hospital room that night.

CHAPTER 19

*M*argie called.

"Hey, Mom. How would it be if I flew down for a visit?"

"Oh, Honey! We'd love it!"

"I'd like to bring Carissa with me."

"Wonderful. What about the boys?"

"Steve has volunteered to be both Mom and Dad so I can come for a couple of days."

"How very brave of him."

"I really want to see Dad."

She didn't add, *one last time*, but I knew she was thinking it.

I had been there after the birth of each of the boys, but when Carissa arrived, a little over a year ago, Bob, although somewhat mobile, could no longer be left alone. He took first priority. Now I was hungry to meet and hold this new life. We set the crib up in Carolyn's bedroom and moved Carolyn into the study.

At thirteen months, Carissa was an elfin creature, with huge, luminous, dark eyes. She stared solemnly at her Grandpa, not quite sure what to make of this person with wheels instead of legs. He solemnly stared back as she capably cruised from couch to chair. Gently we picked her up and placed her in his lap. His arms, unable to automatically enclose her in a protective loving embrace, were placed carefully around her tiny form. We hovered nearby just in case.

The days passed quickly. For us, a glimpse into the life of our new granddaughter. For Margie, a glimpse into the routine that had become our way of life. All too soon, time ran out. As she packed to leave, I walked into the bedroom and put my arms around her.

"Thanks for coming. It meant a great deal for Dad to see you and your precious little girl. She's darling. I really appreciate Steve making it possible for you to come. Give him a big hug from me. I hope the boys haven't been too tough on him."

"Oh, they'll probably all have some interesting stories to tell."

"No doubt, but they surely will have a new appreciation for Mom," I added.

Bob wheeled his chair to the doorway and watched as I carried Carissa out to the car. Margie kissed him goodbye and murmured, "I love you, Daddy." Bob blinked.

Her eyes filled with tears as she climbed into the car.

I leaned in through the open window and gave her a kiss. "What can I say? Thanks. I love you. Call me when you get home."

The car slowly pulled out of the driveway and, with the precious cargo safely buckled in, Carolyn headed for the airport.

The house was unusually still. After a period of profound quiet, Bob's voice seemed to rumble in the silence. "Don't let them forget me."

The words were slurred and difficult to understand, but I knew what he meant. I turned away quickly so he wouldn't see the tears that flooded my eyes.

"Never. You have my solemn pledge."

I crossed the room and rested my head on his arm as I knelt beside his chair.

In mid-December, after four weeks of cautious mouth feeding, we finally were able to get an appointment to have the necessary adjustment made to Bob's feeding tube. Arriving at the hospital, our upbeat outlook quickly turned to dismay when we learned the same doctor who had botched the initial placement was scheduled to make the correction. Although Bob had become infinitely more patient and tolerant in the face of adversity, there was a limit.

"No!" he barked, as he abruptly wheeled his chair around and headed for the door.

Carolyn automatically did an about-face and followed him out to the van while I explained to the receptionist the reason for our quick departure and the need for another appointment with a different radiologist.

In a few more days, we tried again with a different doctor. This time all went well. With the shortened tube now emptying directly into Bob's stomach, his body adjusted quickly to the tube feedings. No more bloating. No more nausea.

There was a shadow looming on the horizon. Because of the additional time required for the tube feeding, the amount of time spent at the office was drastically reduced. Couple that with his unclear speech, and I had serious doubts about the longevity of his employment. When I mentioned it to Bob, he was dismissive.

"Honey, how much longer do you think you should work?"

"Until I stop breathing." (I filled in the missing sounds when he spoke.)

"Right. Seriously, are you able to get much done at the office?"

"Whose side are you on anyway?"

"Your side, of course. But are you pulling your own weight?"

"Granted, things take longer, but my brain still works. Besides the chief said, 'you've got a job here until your body reaches room temperature.' I'm counting on it."

I wasn't so sure. Was he putting too much confidence in words spoken during the initial outpouring of emotion? Had his trusting nature blinded him to the obvious: how long could the company ignore the bottom line? Between Christmas and the New Year we found out.

"Bob, we can't keep you on any longer."

Carolyn and I were seated on either side of Bob, attempting to interpret his speech. But in the end it was to no avail. He was unemployed. Without question, this was the lowest point during his battle with ALS. His mind, still alert, still able to deliberate, was now completely trapped in a body that could no longer move or speak with clarity. His face, robbed of expression by advanced muscle atrophy, displayed neither anger nor despair, but his eyes were filled with anguish. For a man who not only had a passion for his work but spent his life providing for his family, this was a crushing blow.

On New Year's Day, while the rest of the staff enjoyed the day off, we pulled into the empty parking lot. Entering the vacant office, we set about removing the personal items from his desk and shelves along with an assortment of framed pictures and citations. With the exception of an occasional "Does this go?" we worked quietly, saying little.

"What about all these tapes?" I asked, opening a drawer crammed with cassette tapes.

"Leave 'em. Unsolicited audition tapes."

"How about this mic?" During our visit to the station in New York City, Bob spotted a couple of desk microphones from the forties, the Golden Age of Radio. He expressed delight upon seeing them. Soon after we returned to California, one arrived in the mail, cleaned up and looking like new. He was thrilled to get it, and it became the catalyst for many nostalgic conversations about the "good old days."

"It was sent specifically to you."

"Leave it. Let's go."

He turned his chair sharply and headed towards the door. In that moment, he cut the cord. It was over. Forty years of life dedicated to radio broadcasting, and we walked out the door with two boxes. Two boxes. Was that it? You pour your heart and soul into your work, and what do you get? A citation? A word of thanks? Ah, that was the tangible. The intangibles would hover over religious broadcasting for decades. His integrity, his leadership, his reputation would eventually fall like a mantel on son David, who would someday walk in the long shadow cast by his father.

We drove home in silence, knowing that the curtain that had just fallen would soon rise on the final act.

The daily exercise routine continued. One morning after finishing our routine, I sat on the edge of Bob's bed and impulsively picked up his hands and placed them on either side of my face. His eyes lit up and he blinked rapidly while making guttural sounds.

I was shattered. Why hadn't I done this before? For more than a year I had been bathing him, dressing him, feeding him, touching him constantly. It had never occurred to me that he might ache for the touch of my skin under his fingertips. The tears slid down his cheeks and mine as I buried my face in his hands.

Later that day as he sat in the recliner, I settled on the couch next to him.

"Honey," I began somewhat hesitantly, "we have to talk about your cameras."

He looked at me steadily.

"There's so much photographic equipment: cameras, enlargers, a lot of lenses, besides all the darkroom stuff. You've spent a lifetime collecting, using, and keeping everything in mint condition. I know the Leica cameras are sought after, but I haven't any idea of their value, and the other things." I shrugged and shook my head. "Over the years you've had contact with other camera enthusiasts, especially Leica collectors or dealers. Is there anyone you trust who would appreciate what you have?"

He blinked several times.

"Are you up to working on the list today?"

He blinked.

"Want your voice?"

He blinked.

"Okay. Carrie, help me transfer Dad to the wheelchair, and then would you set up his laptop and the switch for Multi-voice?"

"Is it in the office?" she asked.

"Yeah." Looking at Bob I added, "I'll get the inventory list and some of the smaller stuff, like lenses."

He blinked.

While Carolyn worked on one project, I hurried to do mine. The list I found immediately, an undertaking Bob had completed several years ago listing all his photographic equipment. I opened the cupboard and gazed at all the boxes. He had kept the original packing and boxes for almost every piece of equipment. After using anything, he would clean it, place it in the protective padding, and return it to its original box.

There were three exceptions: two enlargers sat on the counter, covered, but too big and heavy to be put away, and one slim Leica I bought for him at an auction with much fear and trepidation because I wasn't even sure it worked. It turned out to be a small treasure. Now it rested in a soft, velvet-like pouch to keep from getting scratched.

As I carefully removed several of the boxes containing lenses, I uncovered a picture propped up against the back wall of the cabinet: a young girl sitting on a log fence. Words clipped from a newspaper had been secured to the photograph with tape now yellowed with age. One, at the bottom of the print, read "Grand" the other, fastened to the top, echoed the phrase of the day, "Slick Chick."

◆　◆　◆

"This is great; lots of places to pose you. How 'bout we start with the fence. Can you climb up and sit on it?"

"Oh, sure."

I dutifully walked across the lawn toward the fence that ran across the back of the property. It was a summer Sunday. I was sixteen; so was Bob.

"Oh, that's good."

I started to climb down.

"No, no. Let me get a couple more just in case it doesn't turn out."

The camera clicked away. "Okay. How about over there by the arbor?" he asked, still holding the camera in front of his face. "Now kinda' reach up and hold onto the arbor," he continued. "Oh, that's gonna' be a good shot."

He knelt down and snapped several pictures.

"Are you done now?"

"Not yet. Let's see. How 'bout the wheelbarrow? Grab the handles as if you are going to pick it up or push it or whatever one does with a wheelbarrow."

I giggled. Click went the camera. I straightened up. "Hey! I wasn't ready!"

"That's when you're the most ready."

I watched while he took several pictures. "You really like taking pictures, don't you?"

"Of you."

"Ah, I know you didn't just run out and buy that camera. You must find some satisfaction in taking pictures."

"Taking the picture is just a little part of it. It's the developing and printing that I really love."

"Where do you do that?" I asked.

"Don't laugh. In the bathroom."

"Oh, I bet the family loves that!"

"They're used to my yelling, 'You can't come in! You'll just have to wait.'"

"So, how did you learn to develop and print pictures, and why do you like it?"

"Mostly on my own. The guys in the camera department are really helpful about getting you started. I suppose they figure it's a hobby and will last a lifetime and you'll spend lots and lots of money to keep it going. And then there are oodles of books and magazines with how-to sections.

"Why do I like it?" He paused. "Nobody ever asked me that before. I suppose there's something very satisfying in developing the negatives; but it's the printing part that's the real head rush. When you expose the negative to a blank piece of photographic paper and immerse it in a chemical bath, the image slowly materializes. It's like magic."

The magic of photography continued. When the children were born, the camera seemed to be a part of Bob. As they grew, if he lifted the camera to his eyes, the children would freeze and smile. After posing for the first shot with that artificial smile, they would loosen up, and then he'd grab a couple more. His love of photography kept him at it long after I would have given up.

When we moved into the Cape Cod with an unfinished basement, number one on the 'to do' list was a darkroom. And so it was that the teen who developed pictures in the bathroom now had his very own darkroom. His cave.

◆　◆　◆

I carefully placed the boxes of lenses on the counter and began to take the cameras out of the cabinet. I slowed; maybe this would be too difficult for him. I remembered when he put these very cameras away for the last time. His fingers had lost strength and dexterity, and he could no longer hold the camera steady enough to take pictures. One by one, he had been forced to give up the "things" that were his persona: driving, photography, speech. I stopped. *Could he do this? Could I? Should we just forget about it? No, it needed to be done.* I picked up a pile of boxes and walked back into the living room, feeling like the wicked witch.

In dealing with my own impending loss, I sometimes forgot the children were also facing the loss of father and grandfather.

When the girls were infants, Bob treated them like porcelain dolls, holding them with the utmost gentleness and fatherly protection. But as the girls matured, he was more than willing to let Mom be the main voice in their lives, finding it rather awkward to discuss female dilemmas. He looked at dating from a male perspective and wasn't quite sure how to react towards muscle-bound gorillas taking his girls out.

He watched them leave for college and was sure they weren't ready. For him, the time between infancy and college had seemingly evaporated overnight and *he* wasn't ready. But, like the adult bird pushing the fledgling out of the nest, when they graduated he encouraged them to make choices and step out on their own, chiding me when I worried about them.

Now, after ten years on her own, Carolyn had returned to lend a helping hand. In the returning, she had reestablished the closeness she shared with her daddy as a small child. Only now, instead of his strong hand steadying her wavering steps, she was supporting him.

David called in January to ask if this would be a good time to visit. I parlayed the question to Bob. "Dave wants to come. Is that okay?"

As if I had to ask. His eyes blinked rapidly.

Bob loved all his children, but, let's face it, there is a special bond that grows between fathers and sons. How do you account for the father-son connection? For Bob it came out of the blue. He'd been through the birthing thing before; he had two daughters. But this time, when the nurse said, "You have a son," the flood of emotion he experienced came as quite a shock.

From the very start there existed a manly bond between father and son that excluded girls. Even during infancy and toddlerhood, dads play differently with boys, more rough and tumble, more aggressive. As David journeyed through his teen years, Bob was quick to support, challenge, or confront accomplishments and behavioral trends. Now, with David married and a family of his own, the father-son bond had blossomed into man-to-man respect.

These visits from the children were merely blips on the radar for we knew that life would return to the dailiness of exercises, feeding tubes, and Bob-care, but each brief visit was a burst of light in the incredibly dark tunnel we all traveled.

CHAPTER 20

*W*hen you go to bed tonight, try to lie there without moving. Unless you have very unusual sleep habits, after about two or three minutes something has to move—even if it's only adjusting your head on the pillow. Bob could not move anything, but his body still had the ability to feel everything. As his muscles atrophied, his body sagged more and more and he quickly became uncomfortable.

His sleep pattern had been disruptive for months, waking every one-and-a-half to two hours and then making noise to awaken me so I could turn him. The intervals of sleep continued to decrease until by early April (month thirty-eight) he was waking every twenty or thirty minutes. Because of his inability to speak, he made guttural sounds to awaken me, and since I fell into a deep sleep after turning him, it became more difficult for him to wake me up.

And that created another problem. Not only was he having trouble staying asleep for an extended period, I was becoming seriously sleep deprived. Carolyn had been spelling me at least once a week, sometimes twice, however, as Bob's condition worsened, he became reluctant to go to sleep without me beside him.

We had been released from the clinic's care a month earlier, but I put in a call to find out if it was safe to give him sleeping medication since his lung function was compromised. Gretchen answered.

"This is Barbara Ball. I have a question about my husband, Bob, who is an ALS patient at the clinic. Can you put me through to someone who knows his case history?"

There was a pause on the other end of the line, and then she blurted out, "My goodness! Is he still alive?"

I was taken aback. I'm sure she hadn't meant it to come out that way, and I wasn't quite sure how to respond. "Well, last time I looked he was."

"Hold on. I'll connect you with the doctor's assistant."

After also expressing some astonishment at Bob's longevity, she asked, "What are you doing with him?"

"I'm not quite sure what you mean."

"Is he at home?"

"Oh, yes."

"Do you have outside help?"

"No. My daughter Carolyn is still helping with him, and we have some really good equipment. We manage."

"Can you tell me what your daily routine is like?"

I gave her a brief summary of our daily activities.

"You mean you're still doing exercises and you get him out of bed and dressed everyday?"

"Well, yeah. Is that bad?"

"Apparently not. Most of our end-stage ALS patients are completely bedridden, so just keep on doing what you're doing. Keep him comfortable and limit any visitors to those who are healthy. No colds or flu."

"Okay. The biggest problem we're having now, and the reason I called, is sleep. He's waking every twenty to thirty minutes because he gets so uncomfortable at night. Is it all right to give him sleeping meds?"

"Oh, of course! At this point give him anything he wants."

We talked a little longer, and then I hung up the phone.

Bob was still a big man. Because of the tube feedings his weight remained fairly constant, around 180. But it was dead weight. Moving him or turning him was increasingly difficult. With his trunk and neck muscles wasted from the disease, he could no longer be transferred from bed to wheelchair without using the lift, and moving him from place to place would have been out of the question if not for the reclining wheelchair to support his head.

Each day as we maneuvered the equipment, we were grateful for the recommendations made by MDA in the early stages of the disease. They knew this day would come; we did not. After getting Bob bathed and dressed each morning while he was still in bed, we got him out of bed with the lift, into the reclining wheelchair, down the hall to the family room (he could no longer operate the chin control), and eventually into the recliner. Most days Bob was content to spend his waking hours in the family room or on the patio, but, thanks to the van, there were still occasional trips to view the nearby ocean.

After such a long illness, visitors expected to find him withering away, confined to bed, and were openly astonished to find him dressed and sitting in the recliner. We were blessed with a handful of faithful friends who stopped by or called or wrote notes. These ongoing contacts bolstered his spirits.

It was the end of the day. Bob sat in the La-Z-Boy recliner, and I sat on the floor in front of him massaging his legs with the electric wand massager. I glanced up at him and encountered his gaze.

I smiled and said, "Let's go to Stanley."

He blinked rapidly.

◆　◆　◆

"Hey, Mom. Guess what?" David asked as he burst into the kitchen after school.

"You're going to run away and join the circus?"

"Close. I've been asked to be drum major for next year," he replied, hunting in the cupboard for something to eat.

"That's quite an honor."

"Oh, I don't know about that. I'm probably the tallest one in the band, and with that towering drum major's hat everybody will be able to see me. But I have to go to Drum Major Camp this summer." He snagged a box of crackers.

"You what? There's a camp for drum majors?"

"Yeah, there really is. They teach you how to march and conduct and use the baton. All that kind of stuff. Do we have any cheese?" He put the box of crackers on the counter.

"In the door of the fridge. When is this camp and how long does it last?"

"Just a minute and I'll tell you." He took the brick of Til-lamook cheddar out of the fridge, set it on the counter, then retrieved a piece of paper from his pocket and the chef's knife from the knife rack. He scanned the paper. "It's, uh, the last week in July, and it's for a week. Oh, yeah, it's at Boise State."

"In Idaho?"

He nodded, focusing his attention on the knife as he continued to slice through the hefty rectangle of cheddar. "Yup. There'll be drum majors, or almost drum majors, from all over the Northwest. We get to stay in the dorm. I need to get this signed by you or Dad if it's okay." He shoved some cheese and crackers in his mouth with one hand and waved the piece of paper at me with the other. I was watching mul-titasking in action.

It had been fourteen years since we traveled through Idaho, so after a brief and enthusiastic interchange with

Bob, we decided to drive Dave to Boise, leave him at drum major's camp, and spend the week camping around Idaho and the Wallowa Mountains in Northeastern Oregon. Really camping. No trailer. No motorhome. Just sleeping bags, a pup tent, and the necessary camping gear.

Near the end of July, armed with maps marked with routes and campsites courtesy of Triple-A of Oregon, we threw our sleeping bags, Coleman stove, ice chest, two-man tent, and all of Dave's gear in the back of the station wagon and set off for Boise. Arriving at the University, we stood by while Dave registered and found his room. Leaving instructions to call the State Police if there was an emergency, we hugged him goodbye and headed for a local motel.

Checking out the next morning, we reserved a room for five days hence and headed for a forest camp in Eastern Oregon. Did we know what we were getting into? Probably not. Two middle-aged people sleeping on the ground, washing with cold water, and cooking on a two-burner stove. Talk about togetherness. It was wonderful.

We saw the Wallowas for the first time—a spectacular mountain range in the northeastern corner of Oregon, often referred to as little "Switzerland of America." One night we camped in the Sawtooth wilderness area of Idaho and were awakened in the morning by a loud clap of thunder.

"Uh-oh," Bob exclaimed, "that sounds like trouble."

There are few things worse than packing a wet tent. Hoping to beat the coming deluge, we flew into action—breaking camp and stowing the last piece of equipment in the station wagon, when, as if on cue, the storm broke. It poured. In the shelter of the car we watched as sheets of water cascaded down the windshield. We slowly pulled away from the campsite and headed towards the main road.

We had no idea where we were going, but we were

looking for breakfast and lots and lots of hot coffee. We ended up at a diner in a little town called Stanley (I'm sure it was the only place to eat for miles), and had the best breakfast ever. Big slabs of ham, eggs done to perfection, cinnamon rolls, and lovely hot coffee. As we were finishing, the rain clouds moved on, pushed along, it seemed, by a much stronger sun.

We were seated at a window. The clouds began to lift, and a panorama of rain-soaked meadow and horses glistening in the brilliant sun came into view. As we admired the pastoral setting, the storm clouds completely lifted, and there was the Sawtooth Range just beyond the meadow—spectacular.

A spontaneous gasp of awe escaped our lips, while at the same moment Bob's hand reached across the table and enclosed mine. We had become part of the scenery transported together into the visual feast that surrounded us. We had gone from dark-gray-can't-see-across-the-street to a moment uniquely frozen in time. A moment we would share as long as we lived.

◆　◆　◆

Although Bob had captured the stunning vista of the Sawtooth Mountains on film, the scene from Stanley was etched forever in our minds. There it would stay to be replayed when things got hectic or stressful.

Life becomes so repetitive, bogged down with meeting the same daily needs, paying the same bills, doing the same job, viewing the same surroundings. Perhaps Wordsworth said it best: "Getting and spending, we lay waste our powers." Looking at it negatively, it seems a treadmill existence with no end in sight. But now, as Bob's body was steadily dying with Lou Gehrig's, that very dailiness of life, unseen and largely forgotten, became the foundation that enabled us to recall the magical moments we were privileged to share. Most of them unplanned and unexpected, but part of our lives forever.

Like the snowstorm we encountered near midnight as we drove over the Santiam Pass in Oregon's Cascade Mountains. It was November, and, at that late hour, we seemed to be the only ones foolhardy enough to be on the road. The snowplow was at least a mile ahead of us, and, by the time we reached the summit, a fresh coating of undisturbed snow covered everything.

We traveled on a bed of pristine whiteness surrounded by a forest of evergreens, branches heavy with snow. The headlights revealed a world of startling brilliance as big flakes continued their silent fall. Everything was hushed. The road itself asleep under a blanket of spotless white. For those few minutes, as we cautiously crept over the summit, we became part of the surroundings. Alone in a world of shimmering radiance. We were mute with wonder, as if a sound from either of us would break the spell. Those are the moments you cherish, the unique memories you share.

We had finished the morning workout when Bob indicated he wanted the alphabet chart. I held it in front of him and spelled out the letters one by one as his gaze fell on them.

"I?"

He blinked

"T, it?"

Blink.

"W?"

Blink.

"O?"

Blink.

"N?"

Blink.

"T, won't?"

Blink.

"B?"

Blink.

"E, be?"

Blink.

"L?"

Blink.

"O?"

Blink.

"N?"

Blink.

"G, long?"

Blink.

"N?"

Blink.

"O?"

Blink.

"W" I crumpled down on the edge of the bed and grabbed his hands. "No. I'm not ready to let you go."

The words just tumbled out of my mouth and hung there like little dark clouds. What a selfish thing to say. But it was true. We knew from the start this was a fatal disease, but it was an ambiguous fatal, somewhere off there in the future. Now I had to face the reality of fatal. Soon.

I cradled his cheek in my hand and murmured, "I'm sorry, Honey, I love you so very much. I'll never be ready."

The elephant was back. I suppose he had been there all along, but I had become so used to his presence I barely noticed him anymore. Now he brought the smell of death.

Lord, I'm so weary. I need sleep. Give me the strength to get through just one more night and then I'll call the nurse and see if we can arrange to have someone spell me a couple nights each week.

I can't believe I just thought that. In the vast scheme of things this is just a hiccup. There will be time enough to catch up on sleep. I can certainly hold out. On the other hand, I'm not going to be any help if Bob can't waken me at night with his soft guttural sounds. As the day wore on, I became more convinced we'd get through one more night and then I'd talk to him about getting some help.

It was after four in the afternoon. Bob had been showing signs of distress throughout the day. His breathing was becoming increasingly labored, even though a cannula, inserted into his nostrils and connected to a small canister, provided a steady supply of oxygen.

"Would you like me to call the doctor and see if he would stop by on his way home?"

Bob blinked and then grunted several times.

"You want the alphabet chart?"

He blinked.

I picked it up off the table and held it in front of him.

"N?"

He blinked.

"O?"

He blinked and looked at me.

"No?"

Blink.

"H?"

Blink.

"O?"

Blink.

"S?"

Blink.

"P?"

Blink.

"Hospital?" I guessed at the word.

He blinked.

"Honey, they'd have to tromp over me to get you. No way will I let them stick you in the hospital." Then I added, "But, if you want, you can still change your mind and go on a ventilator."

He turned his gaze back to the alphabet.

"N?"

He blinked.

"And I suppose that stands for No?"

Blink.

I bent and kissed his cheek. "It's been a long haul. I'll give the doctor a call."

I called Dr. Hedstrom and explained the situation.

"I've got a medical symposium after hours, but I'll stop by about eight-thirty or nine if that's not too late."

"We'll be up. Thanks, Doc."

It took so long to move Bob and get him settled that we usually started winding down and heading towards bed between nine-thirty and ten p.m. It was now almost ten, and no sign of Dr. Hedstrom.

"I'm thinking he is not going to show," I began. "We really need to get you," my words were interrupted by the phone ringing. "Ah, guess who that is."

I grabbed the phone on the second ring. "Hello?"

"Barbara, this is Dr. Hedstrom. Things here are still in session. It will probably be another thirty minutes or so. Will you be up that long?"

I looked at Bob. His eyes were half shut. He needed to get to bed.

"We were just heading to bed. Could you call in the morning?"

"Of course. I'm sorry this didn't work out. I'll call tomorrow."

I hung up the phone and turned to Bob. "Hedstrom is still in meetings. He'll call tomorrow morning to see how you're doing. So, let's shuttle you off to bed. Want a couple sips of iced tea?"

He blinked.

The evening routine was like the morning, only in reverse. When Bob was finally in the hospital bed, I raised it to an angled sitting position and carefully poured about a spoonful of iced tea into his mouth. Unable to swallow, most of it dribbled out unto the towel I had draped around him, but a little ran down his throat. After a few small tastes, I cleaned him up, lowered the bed, got him comfortably settled, and kissed him good night. I quickly got myself ready for bed and by eleven-fifteen the house was dark. I lay next to Bob in bed, listening to his labored breathing, and wondering how I could possibly tell this man I loved it was time to get some outside help. Maybe Hedstom would do it.

I woke with a start. The numbers on the clock glowed 2:07.

"No. No." I knew what those numbers meant. I hadn't slept this long in months. It was ominously still. I reached out my hand and touched Bob's face. It was icy.

"Oh, Bob. You've left me."

Death.

It comes to everyone. Rich and poor, saint and sinner, famous and infamous, we all have one thing in common: we die. We glance at the obituaries without a twinge. Death is commonplace until it invades my home, my family, my loved ones. Then and only then do we feel its sting.

Tears slid down my cheeks. Ironic that I was no longer concerned about sleep, but this was not the solution I had in mind. I sat cross-legged on my bed and stroked his head. "You're free, now. Loosed from this house of flesh that held you captive for so long.

At this very moment you're standing on your own two feet before the throne of God singing praises with your strong bass voice that was silent for so long. And someday, by His grace and in His time, I'll stand there with you." The tears continued to fall.

In the dim glow of the nightlight, a slight movement near the peak of the vaulted ceiling caused me to look up. A gentle stirring. Angels? God's messengers come to escort Bob home? Perhaps. Something was there, and then all was still.

In the wee hours of the morning a blessed hush seemed to have fallen over the house. Quietly I showered and dressed and then sat beside Bob's bed waiting for dawn, waiting to awaken Carolyn so she could say goodbye to her daddy in privacy. I marveled at how quietly he had slipped away, no choking, no gasping. A fragment of the lyrics from an old song whispered through my head:

> Softly, I will leave you softly,
> Long before you miss me,
> Long before your arms can beg me stay
> For one more hour or one more day.

The love of my life was gone and my heart ached with the magnitude of that loss. A part of me was gone forever, and I was left with a giant, gaping hole. For Bob, the ordeal of watching his own life slip away was over and he now found himself rejoicing in the presence of Christ his Saviour. In that I took comfort.

For me a new journey was beginning, and I would travel the road without my soulmate by my side. I looked down the path that lay ahead with some apprehension, but, just as we sought God's guidance when we began our life together, I knew I would continue to seek His face. He who promised to go before me and never leave me nor forsake me would surely guide my footsteps.

I could rest in the assurance that God's promises never fail.

EPILOGUE

*W*e were going on a cruise, the whole family.

Because of prior commitments, Bob had to make a business stop first, so I helped him pack and saw him off a day early. We would get things ready and leave by 4:30 the next afternoon in order to meet Bob at the dock in time for the cruise departure.

Next day we fooled around at various projects, not corporately, individual busy-ness, but we were aware of each other's presence. Late in the morning, I went for a walk.

I checked my watch. It was almost three o'clock. I hurried up the driveway to the house. As I drew closer, I realized we had done little to prepare to leave, and we had to leave by 4:30. No packing was done, the mail had not been stopped, and I hadn't even gotten anyone to look after the house or the cat. I walked faster, then I began to run. I burst into the house and yelled, "Quick! We have to be out of here by 4:30!"

The girls were nowhere to be found. The enormity of the situation crashed in upon me as I recognized the hopeless task we faced.

I was wide-eyed awake. This was no morning of lazy wakefulness. The dream had seemed so real that the panic I felt upon awakening was just beginning to subside. I tried to put the disturbing dream in perspective. What, if anything, did this vision in the night mean?

Bob had been gone for more than a year.

He had gone on ahead.

We would meet him later.

But the here and now often seemed overwhelming and I faced it without him.

It's been ten years now, ten years of living on my own, ten years of making decisions without Bob. What I've discovered about myself in those ten years is that the person I am now is part Bob. I will never be the pre-Bob me, nor would I want to be. He helped make me complete, to give me a fuller, richer life. "Widow," I've decided, is only a designation you circle on forms. I still feel married. Do I still miss him? Every day. And during those moments when the ache of loneliness creeps in, I seek the face of the One who gives hope beyond the grave.

The God whose promises never fail.

The God who protects and defends the widow.

The God who holds my breath in His hand.

My God.

And that is enough.

AFTERWARDS

*D*id you know every time the clock ticks away 90 minutes someone in the US is diagnosed with ALS? And in that same brief interval of 90 minutes ALS claims another life.

Every 90 minutes.

Research to find the cause of ALS and discover an effective treatment continues. Current technology has made it possible to share research data and subsequent findings in a timely manner and on an international basis.

If you would like to have a part in the search for the cause and cure of this deadly disease, please contact either of the organizations listed below. Your support on behalf of those fighting ALS is greatly appreciated. Thank you.

The ALS Association
27001 Agoura Road, Suite 250
Calabasas Hills, CA 91301-9817

Muscular Dystrophy Association
ALS Division
3300 E Sunrise Drive
Tucson, AZ 85718